A MONSTER
AT THE TOP OF THE TREE
How To Make Your Own Family Tree

Who are you?
What sort of family did you come from?
How do you fit into history?

One of the best ways of finding out is to build your own *Family Tree*.

Everyone has a great choice of ancestors. We have all had two parents, four grandparents, eight great-grandparents, sixteen great-great-grandparents. In this way the branches of a family tree spread and carry us backwards.

This book shows you how to build your own family tree and shows some of the unusual characters the author met when she built up her Family Tree.

4 cde

D1428562

To Langdon my husband with love and gratitude, and to
the memory of my father who would have been so
amused by it all.

A MONSTER AT THE TOP OF THE TREE
HOW TO MAKE YOUR OWN FAMILY TREE
A CAROUSEL BOOK 0 552 54083 8

First publication in Great Britain 1975

PRINTING HISTORY
Carousel edition published 1975

Text Copyright © 1975 by Kathleen Menhinick Dewey
Illustrations copyright © Transworld Publishers Ltd. 1975

Carousel Books are published by Transworld Publishers Ltd.,
Cavendish House, 57–59 Uxbridge Road,
Ealing, London, W.5

Made and printed in Great Britain by
Cox & Wyman Ltd., London, Reading and Fakenham

A MONSTER AT THE TOP OF THE TREE

How to Make Your Own Family Tree

KATHLEEN MENHINICK DEWEY
Illustrated by EDWARD MORTELMANS

TRANSWORLD PUBLISHERS LTD

ACKNOWLEDGEMENT

Heartfelt thanks are due to my cousin, the Rev. Thomas Shaw, who did so much of the groundwork, and to my husband Langdon, who drew up the charts and helped in the arduous research. I should like also to thank my son and daughter-in-law for their valuable assistance on several occasions.

FOREWORD

A cousin of the author's by marriage, a clergyman living in Cornwall, became interested in his wife's unusual maiden name, which happened to be Menhinick, and decided to do some research. His studies took him far afield and brought many surprises. The further he went the more fascinating it became. From his findings this book developed.

CONTENTS

INTRODUCTION

Have you ever wondered about your family? It is really quite exciting to know who you are, what sort of family you come from, and how you fit into history. One of the best ways of recording any individual's place in the scheme of things is to write a *Family History* or to build up a *Family Tree*. A Tree is really a chart or diagram showing all the human or blood connections of the person concerned.

Making a Family Tree

Imagine that you are the trunk of the Tree, then the side branches may be your brothers and sisters and this includes their children if they have any, who are your nephews and nieces. Then come the higher branches which contain the names of your father and mother, each of whom had two parents who are your grand-parents.

This book reveals some of the stories which came to light as one particular Family Tree grew. With each generation the pattern grows ever more complicated. This pattern can be shown either in chart form (the branches of the Tree) or as a written Family History. The charts at the end of each chapter in this book show how far the branches spread. The author begins with her earliest memories and gradually builds up her own Family History.

Specific instructions are given at the end of each chapter for writing a *Family History* and for making a *Family Tree*.

1

MYSELF

I LEARNED quite early that there had always been farmers in my family. When I was a little girl I lived in an old, old house called oddly enough New Hall. It is situated near Wareside in Hertfordshire. It was first built in 1326 and was a monastery belonging to the monks of the Holy Cross. In the Middle Ages, when New Hall was built, the monks would have fed the poor, healed the sick, and have made beautiful books by hand before printing was invented. Not much of the earliest building remains, but we always spoke of the brewhouse and the bakehouse instead of a kitchen or a scullery. My brother Jack and I played in a chapel with a stained-glass window instead of in a nursery. The four children who are growing up now at New Hall are no relation to me, but their parents always give me a warm welcome when I call. I have watched these boys playing badminton in the monks' chapel.

Experts are visiting New Hall to search out the older parts. Small doorways with narrow pointed arches, which have been plastered over, are being discovered. In the garden are the remains of a moat. These moats or ponds used to surround a house completely and served as protection against invasion. There was a font in the hall which would have held water for the monks when they crossed themselves. I can remember when I could not reach the font even on tiptoe, but now it only comes up to my waist. There was a lofty cedar growing in the garden. I used to think that its branches touched the floor of Heaven. Now only a stump remains, thirty-six inches across, which shows the great age of the tree.

There were no monks there in our day. New Hall had become a farmhouse and my father was a farmer. We employed several men and boys to help us outdoors and my mother had a maid and a companion-help; this was a young woman who lived as one of the family to help look after us children, rather like an au pair girl at the present time. Life was very comfortable then for people in the middle-class.

Our lives were pleasant though we did not have a bathroom and we cooked on a kitchen range. At night we carried lighted candles to our beds and these used to throw strange shadows on the walls. Now there are three bathrooms at New Hall. Main water and electricity have at last reached these remote villages. Though there were no buses and we had no car, we did not feel isolated. We drove to market or to visit our friends with a pony and trap, and every day a horse and cart carrying milk churns went to the town of Ware three miles away. Our milk was sold to a factory which made baby foods. My father was a wonderful driver; he would click his tongue and the pony would trot gaily along those peaceful roads, where few cars came to frighten him. Later

my brother and I had bicycles and we would sail down steep hills like the wind. Another favourite pastime was to wander into the meadows to pick cowslips in spring, or blackberries in the mellow autumn sunshine.

In August Jack and I enjoyed going into the harvest fields to watch the corn being cut. In those days a binder was used. This cut the barley or wheat and tied it into sheaves which were then set up by a man with a hand fork so that they could dry in pyramids called stooks or shocks. We used to chat with the men as they ate their lunch. Our favourite worker, Pickles, who died recently at ninety, could eat a whole rabbit pie by himself, which filled us with admiration. Once I ran in front of the binder to see if I could race it. The driver put me firmly on a sheaf. 'You sit there, Missy; if harm came to you the guv'nor would never forgive me.'

How different a harvest field looks today. The wheat is cut and threshed all in one operation by a huge combine, so that the grain is ready for the market much earlier. Fewer workers are required. My younger relations employ perhaps only two men, whereas in my childhood there would have been a dozen.

Now I belong to another kind of family which looks forward to the future. My parents are long since dead, so too is my brother Jack, but I am not alone. I have a husband Langdon, a grown-up son, Adrian, a daughter-in-law Ann and a baby granddaughter, Helen Guinevere. My brother left some descendants also: two sons, Leonard and David, and Leonard's teenage sons Kevin and Stephen.

*   *   *

Writing a Family History

You can begin with yourself and your early life, as far back as your memory can stretch. Someone centuries hence may be interested to know how you lived, what clothes you wore, what you had to eat, and how you passed your leisure time.

When you wish to go further back in time you could question your oldest living relatives before they die and take much precious information with them. If these people do not live near send a polite letter. I am sure that they will help you.

An important source of information is a family Bible which has names and dates of births on a special page. There may be other family documents or records such as diaries, letters or newspaper cuttings.

If you live in an old house you may be able to find out its history from your County Reference Library. You may like to illustrate your account with family photographs.

Chart 1

Beginning a Tree

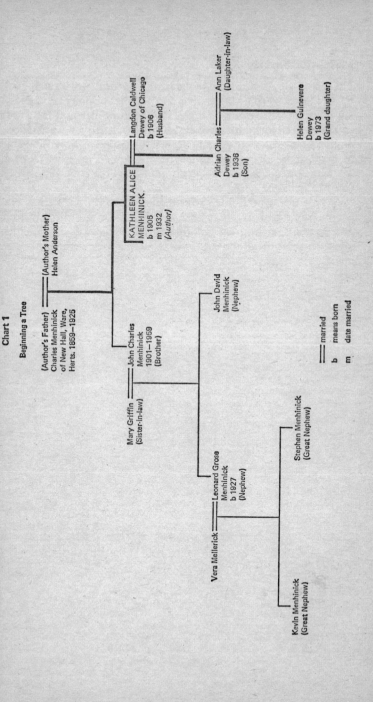

(Author's Father)
Charles Menhinick
of New Hall, Ware,
Herts, 1859–1925
══ (Author's Mother)
Helen Anderson

KATHLEEN ALICE
MENHINICK
b 1905
m 1932
(Author)
══ Langdon Caldwell
Dewey of Chicago
b 1906
(Husband)

Ann Laker
(Daughter-in-law)

Adrian Charles
Dewey
b 1936
(Son)

Helen Guinevere
Dewey
b 1973
(Grand daughter)

Mary Griffin
(Sister-in-law)
══ John Charles
Menhinick
1901–1959
(Brother)

John David
Menhinick
(Nephew)

Vera Mellerick
══ Leonard Grose
Menhinick
b 1927
(Nephew)

Stephen Menhinick
(Great Nephew)

Kevin Menhinick
(Great Nephew)

══ married
b means born
m date married

Making a Family Tree

Take a sheet of drawing paper from an ordinary sketch pad,
7″ × 11″ or 8″ × 10″. Make a diagram like the one on page 11 showing yourself, your brothers and sisters and mother and father. If
you are already an aunt or uncle include your nephews and nieces.
As the Tree grows more branches will be added. You will be able
to make more diagrams, which can be joined together as each
branch is traced. So it will spread until the Tree is as complete as
you can make it.

A Tree begins to branch with mother and father. As these two
people each had a father and mother, there are already four
grandparents, eight great grandparents and so on. Always include
interesting brothers and sisters of your parents, your aunts and
uncles.

2

FIRST BRANCHES: MOTHER

MY mother, Helen Anderson, who came from Scotland, was a pretty woman with a pale, clear-cut face, but she was delicate. She had a fine well-trained singing voice and often sang Scottish ballads at local concerts. She did beautiful embroidery and was a wonderful cook, not only baking shortbread and other Scottish delicacies, but providing Cornish splits and yeast cake as well. She was skilful too at the game of croquet which was fashionable then, and would often win, which we children thought unfair.

Not long ago one of my English cousins told me that he had always admired my mother, his aunt-in-law, very much. 'She was my idea of a perfect lady, so serene and gracious.' This made me happy because I remembered that ill-health had brought her much sorrow and weariness. She died at fifty-four of a blood disease which

can be cured now. She always retained a deep love for
Scotland, her own country, and took us north, year after
year, to visit her mother and sister.

It was from these ladies, my aunts and my Scottish
grandmother, that I learned many things about that
side of the family. My grandfather, John Anderson, who
died before my parents married, had been a tall handsome man with thick curly hair and beard, which later
became snow-white. He too was a farmer like my father,
but they lived in a different style of house. It was built of
solid grey granite and was not as ancient as New Hall,
but it occupied a commanding position in a fertile part
of Aberdeenshire. In the distance rose the mountain
Bennachie which I have climbed. There were fewer trees
in their landscape and the winds in winter were bitterly
cold.

John was born in 1821, the year Napoleon died. He
had been one of a large family, but all his brothers and
sisters died of scarlet fever in infancy; a killing disease in
those days. John became an Elder in the Scottish Kirk
(church) and was respected far and wide. An Elder is
someone in a Scottish church who helps the minister and
visits the people in their homes. Nowadays women too
can be Elders.

When he was over forty John married Maggie Davidson, a beautiful girl of eighteen who became my grandmother. She had brown eyes and auburn hair; her face
was oval with a bright, clear complexion and an ex-
pression of great sweetness. There are many stories told
of men being smitten by her charms, though she was no
flirt; indeed rather serious and mature for her age. At
her boarding-school not only the teachers but the other
pupils addressed her as Miss Davidson. We are much less
formal today.

There was the story of the medical student who

walked twenty-four miles from Aberdeen University to call on her. There were no cars then or motor-bicycles and evidently he could not afford to keep a horse. The

story I like best concerns the elderly neighbour who stopped the newly-wedded pair as they left the kirk a few days after their marriage. Maggie was wearing a crinoline and a bonnet instead of a hat to denote her new status. 'Auchnieve, Auchnieve, I just wonder that she took ye. Ye wouldna' see the like of her from Dan to Beersheba.' Dan and Beersheba are towns in the Holy Land. Images from the Bible were part of everyday speech in those Scottish circles. Notice that my grandfather was not called John or Mr. Anderson, but Auchnieve, the name of the farm which his family had occupied for two hundred years. This had long been a Scottish custom and continues to this day.

Though John and Maggie had eight children they gave them all a good education. Two of my aunts went to school in Germany and then to Aberdeen University. In Scotland there has always been a strong drive towards learning.

From my aunts I learned about a very distinguished member of the family: Thomas Davidson, the Wandering Scholar. He had been an older half-brother of my grandmother, and thus was my great-uncle. He died in 1900, the year of my parents' marriage. How thrilled I was to hear about this man and wished so much that I could have met him. Two biographies or life-stories have been written about him. He could speak twelve languages fluently and travelled widely. He adopted his title from the Wandering Scholars of the Middle Ages, whom he much admired. He went to America and founded the Breadwinners' College, which was a school for poor immigrants arriving in this new country without money or friends. He wanted to help them to learn English and obtain an education. A magazine called the Spectator claimed that he was one of the twelve most learned men alive at that time in the world.

Thomas knew many of the famous people of the day, including Heinrich Schliemann who dug up the ancient city of Troy. He became friendly with William Morris, an artist who was reviving an interest in all kinds of handcraft, including tapestry and carpet weaving. Together they founded the *Fellowship of the New Life*. This was a movement to help people live unselfishly, according to high ideals.

What I honour most in my great-uncle is that he

cared nothing for money or fame, and turned down offers of brilliant jobs. He only wanted to help others to lead fuller lives. When he went to Rome he spoke Latin with the Pope who declared himself amazed at the learning of this Scotsman. He never married, it was said, because the sweetheart of his youth died early and he could not replace her. He would often recite poetry in a deep vibrant voice. He was especially fond of Tennyson's *In Memoriam* which he knew by heart.

My aunts would also tell me about Sir Robert Davidson who was provost of Aberdeen in 1411, and who led the Lowlanders against the Highlanders, defeating them at the Battle of Harlaw. He is supposed to be an ancestor, but this they could not directly prove. In Aberdeen Cathedral there is a sword belonging to Sir Robert which they took me to see.

Writing a Family History: Mother

Study family photograph albums, question closely all the living relatives, especially the older ones. Again study a Family Bible, if you have one, and old letters and diaries.

Making a Family Tree: Maternal Line

Again using a piece of paper 7″ × 11″ or 8″ × 10″ make a chart of your mother's family. Show her parents and grandparents and if possible her aunts and uncles. This can be joined to your first chart, where it belongs.

References used in this chapter

Much information came from mother's relatives, her sisters, her aunt and her own mother.

A book called *Memorials of Thomas Davidson* edited by William Knight (1907) is now in the author's possession.

Information about William Morris, friend of Davidson, was found in the Encyclopedia Britannica.

The Dictionary of National Biography edited by Sir Leslie

Stephen and Sir Sidney Lee, published by the *Oxford University Press* and in London by *Humphrey Milford*. This work comprises twenty-two volumes and six supplements. It is available in Public Reference Libraries, and contains much detail about well-known historical figures.

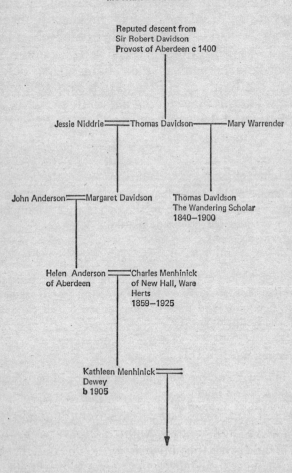

Chart 2

MOTHER'S BRANCH

Reputed descent from
Sir Robert Davidson
Provost of Aberdeen c 1400

Jessie Niddrie══════Thomas Davidson─────────Mary Warrender

John Anderson══════Margaret Davidson   Thomas Davidson
                                          The Wandering Scholar
                                          1840–1900

Helen Anderson ═══════Charles Menhinick
of Aberdeen   of New Hall, Ware
                       Herts
                       1859–1925

Kathleen Menhinick═══════
Dewey
b 1905

3

FIRST BRANCHES: FATHER

MY Cornish father, Charles Menhinick, was forty-six when I was born, but to me he always seemed young and vigorous, even up to the week of his death when he was sixty-six. He was of middle height, sturdily built with a ruddy complexion; he had iron grey hair and dark grey eyes. Before his marriage he had lived in Russia where he had managed the estate of a wealthy countess; a lady who might have stepped straight out of Tolstoy's famous novel *War and Peace*. Though he was a farmer he had wide interests outside his job and was a voracious reader. I can still hear him declaiming aloud the *Hebrew Melodies* of Byron, his favourite poet, or some of Shakespeare's stirring speeches. He had a great sense of humour and would often tease me because I was dreamy and unpractical. He used to say that I would be late on the Day of Judgment, but when I brought good reports home from school he was delighted. He was determined that I should go to the university which he had missed in his youth because he had been one of a large family.

Charles took up public work, became chairman of the Rural District Council, a County Councillor and a magistrate. When I smashed up my first bicycle he went straight out to buy me a new one. Once when I had bad earache he walked to the chemist in the middle of the night. One does not easily forget a father who was so kind.

The Cornish Menhinicks, my father's forbears, followed a long tradition of farming. Some were tenant farmers, others were yeomen farmers, that is men farming their own land. Others again had been stone-masons and some had been inn-keepers. Some were very well-to-do, others were receiving what we should now call social security. Some of the Menhinicks emigrated to America, others to Canada, Australia and New Zealand. Their descendants, all claiming a Cornish origin, were happy to correspond with us and fill in details of the family history. About sixty years ago a Red Indian chief came to visit the President of the United States. He wanted to make a complaint about his 'reservation', the land on which he had been forced to live. His name was . . . John Menhinick. Did he adopt that name from some wandering Cornish settler? I should love to know.

The name Menhinick, which originally came from a place called Menegby Nyot, is found all over Cornwall in parish registers where dates of baptisms, marriages and burials are entered. It is also found on tombstones. Public libraries sometimes have copies of these registers, which are easier to read.

All these sources reveal that my direct ancestor was Richard Menhinick who married Katherine Lander in 1579, thus taking the name back through ten generations. Before that time no Menhinick had owned Land. I like to think of a solid farmer, bearing my name, ploughing his fields, milking his cows and turning the milk into rich Cornish cream, while Shakespeare was acting in the theatre and writing plays. Richard would have spoken Cornish which is now a forgotten language, but was akin to Welsh, and he would have thought of London as very far away. In some Cornish churches you still find the Lord's prayer written in the ancient language. I should like to learn it but I do not know how it should be pronounced.

A helpful factor in compiling this story was the Menhinick habit of keeping diaries and writing descriptions of important events in their lives, not for publication but for their own interest and amusement. Some of them were kind enough to let us use these notes.

The great-great-great-grandson of the first Richard Menhinick was Alexander, born in 1738 and a skilled stone-mason. These stone-masons were much in demand for the building of monuments and tombstones. In 1770 he laid aside his mallet, chisel and trowel, bought some land and became a prosperous farmer. He felt that now he was rich enough to be his own boss and to walk with pride over his own fertile acres. His home *Tregarden*, a small mansion, has been called a poem in Cornish stone.

The gateway bears the date 1631, but the mullioned windows are older still. This Alexander became a church warden. Every Sunday he would ride to church and tie his horse to the hitching post provided.

One lovely spring day in 1785 Alexander was sitting in his pew when suddenly he heard the name of his nineteen year old daughter Elizabeth spoken aloud. Her banns in marriage were being called and he had no idea that she was even engaged. He had to sit quietly there because as church warden he was obliged to take up and count the collection. But inwardly he was fuming with rage because he did not approve of the young man, a poor carpenter, whom he considered beneath him, now that he was a person of some importance in the district.

When the service was over Alexander leapt upon his horse and galloped home with all speed, only to find that Elizabeth had fled. She had taken refuge with her uncle John, a stalwart stone-mason over six feet tall. Her uncle's wife Sarah was called upon to give advice. She told her niece that having put her hand to the plough she must not look back. So Elizabeth married her carpenter, but through the good offices of her uncle was later reconciled to her father, who was my great-great-great-grandfather. It was Elizabeth's grandson, a Mr. Pollard, who retold the story over a century after the event, so the quaint little incident has come down to us today.

In the late eighteenth century conditions were harsh for the poor in England. The industrial revolution was just beginning. Wages were low, houses were insanitary. Tin miners in Cornwall were drunken and ignorant; often cruel to their wives and children. Into this unhappy scene came John Wesley, a powerful and eloquent preacher who longed to help people to lead better lives and be kinder to each other. He succeeded in

changing the habits and morals of whole villages over-
night; by his winning words he found a way to touch the
hardest hearts. His regular habits of prayer, beginning
at four a.m., gave to him and his followers the nickname
of Methodists. Riding on horseback John Wesley visited
the duchy of Cornwall thirty-two times in all, and had a
powerful impact upon everyone he met. My own family
embraced with enthusiasm this more emotional and intense version of Christianity, which was sweeping
through Cornwall like a forest fire. The Cornish have
always been ruggedly individual and like to 'do their
own thing' as people say now, in religion as in other
ways.

Among the sons of the Alexander Menhinick whose
daughter eloped was another Alexander, my great-great
great-uncle, nicknamed the Perfect Christian by his
friends and neighbours, and whose life-story was written
up in the Methodist Magazine of 1819. This man, who
was only thirty-seven when he died in 1812, became
himself an eloquent preacher. Methodists have always
made much use of lay men, whom they call local preach-
ers, to carry on the work of their church. Alexander
was busy during the week in the grocer's shop which he
owned, but was always ready to ride on horseback
Sunday after Sunday to take services in remote wayside
chapels. He was no sour killjoy but a man always smiling
and full of zest for life. Everyone loved him.

There are anecdotes which describe Alexander pull-
ing golden sovereigns from his purse to give to those in
need. 'Friend, you look dejected,' he would say to some
poor man he had met, 'would this little gift help you?'
One does not see sovereigns now but I remember them
very well. A sovereign was supposed to be a pound but
bought far more than a pound note at the present day. I
should have enjoyed meeting this kind uncle when he

was giving his money away so freely. He was an affectionate husband, a good father to his four children (one daughter later married the mayor of Penzance) and a generous employer to the servants and apprentices who worked for him.

In those days maid-servants were plentiful in Cornwall for there were no factories or offices in which girls could work. Alexander would have had two or three young apprentices in his care; lads bound for a term of years to work for him and so learn the grocery trade. Twice a day Alexander would conduct Family Prayers behind the shop for this enlarged household. The prayers, which he wrote out in his account book and which survive today, were warm and sincere, coming from the heart.

As we travel forwards in time we find that this intense religious feeling has persisted among the Menhinicks for several generations. My grandfather Alexander Menhinick was considered a fine preacher, and his brother Charles, my great-uncle, had the reputation of being a fiery, eloquent expounder of the Christian gospel. My brother Jack, following in his father's footsteps, became a magistrate, a County Councillor and chairman of his own Rural District Council in Essex. I myself have preached regularly in a Methodist church and have been trained for social work.

*   *   *

Writing a Family History: Father

The sources are the same as before: the oldest living relatives, perhaps a Family Bible, parish records, the local church register of births, marriages and burials. Local histories in your *Reference Library*.

Making a Family Tree: Paternal Line

Make a separate diagram of your father's branch, tracing your father's ancestors as far back as possible. This is the paternal line. Join to earlier charts at the appropriate place.

Beginning with readily available information about father's family through the memories of living relatives, Family Bibles, etc., it was possible to work back through Parish Registers, records of wills and then into further specialized reference works such as the *History of Trigg Minor*. It was through this intensive far-flung research that the name of this farming family, the Cornish Menhinicks, was at last traced back to 1579.

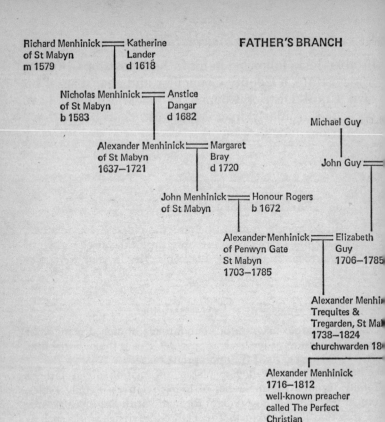

FATHER'S BRANCH

Richard Menhinick of St Mabyn m 1579 ═══ Katherine Lander d 1618

Nicholas Menhinick of St Mabyn b 1583 ═══ Anstice Dangar d 1682

Michael Guy

Alexander Menhinick of St Mabyn 1637–1721 ═══ Margaret Bray d 1720

John Guy ═══

John Menhinick of St Mabyn ═══ Honour Rogers b 1672

Alexander Menhinick of Penwyn Gate St Mabyn 1703–1785 ═══ Elizabeth Guy 1706–1785

Alexander Menhi... Trequites & Tregarden, St Ma... 1738–1824 churchwarden 18...

Alexander Menhinick 1716–1812 well-known preacher called The Perfect Christian

Chart 3

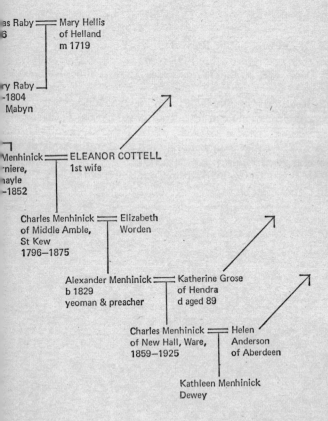

Phillips

hillips

as Raby ══════ Mary Hellis
6   of Helland
                 m 1719

ry Raby ──┐
-1804
  Mabyn

──┐
Menhinick ══════ ELEANOR COTTELL
niere,   1st wife
ayle
-1852

    Charles Menhinick ══════ Elizabeth
    of Middle Amble,   Worden
    St Kew
    1796–1875

        Alexander Menhinick ══════ Katherine Grose
        b 1829   of Hendra
        yeoman & preacher   d aged 89

            Charles Menhinick ══════ Helen
            of New Hall, Ware,   Anderson
            1859–1925   of Aberdeen

                Kathleen Menhinick
                Dewey

References used in this chapter

St. Mabyn's Church Registers
St. Mabyn's Rate Book
Other Cornish Parish Registers
Wills of Bodmin Probate Court
Bodmin Guardian File, Bodmin Public Library (now known as Social Security)
Family Bibles
Methodist Magazine of 1819

General:

Records of the Society of Genealogists in London British Museum

1851 Census returns, Public Record Office, London

History of Trigg Minor by Sir John Maclean 1873 three volumes. (This book was available on order from Public Reference Libraries.)

A Parish Register is usually kept locked in the church vestry. Ask your local vicar if you can trace your name back as far as it can go. Sometimes there is a fee charged for this service. This research will be easier if your family has lived in the same place for several generations.

Local Rate Books are available from County Record Office. Apply to the County Archivist.

PATERNAL GRANDMOTHER

SO far I have spoken about three grandparents: my mother's father and mother and their relations, and my father's paternal line, the Cornish Menhinicks. But remember that everyone has four grandparents. I had a Cornish grandmother, Katherine or Kitty Menhinick, my father's mother, who lived to be eighty-nine and whom I loved very much. She was not as pretty as Maggie Anderson, but she was dignified and stately. Both ladies always wore ankle-length black dresses, stiff white starched caps with long floating streamers on their heads and white lace shawls on their shoulders. This attire showed that they were widows. Grandmothers in those days were a race apart; now they look like everyone else. Kitty was a well-read woman who liked to recite poetry aloud. I too love poetry, so I often felt very close to her. My own mother was a more practical woman; skilled in cooking and needlework. Kitty used to read a Bible with huge print because her eyes had begun to fail. This filled me with awe. It must be an important book, I thought, if people took all that trouble to read it.

My grandmother's maiden name was Grose and her mother's name, before she became Mrs. Grose, had been Rebecca Male. These families were neighbours in Cornwall to the Menhinicks; some were farmers and some were master-builders. The Groses originally spelt their name as Grosse, which is a French word meaning fat or big, and they had been Quakers before they became Methodists. In 1677 Ambrose Grosse, a direct ancestor of Kitty, had goods valued at £26 (a vast sum in those days) taken from him because he attended a Quaker meeting, and in the following year 1678 he lost all his cattle because he insisted upon worshipping God in his own way.

The Quakers were a body of people far ahead of their time. They were opposed to men being hanged for sheep-stealing, they fought against the slave trade, and when they emigrated to America they did no harm to the Red Indians, unlike some other European settlers. They have always hated violence and cruelty. All this information we found in a series of books called the *Sufferings of the Friends ...* in the various counties. The volume we asked our County Library to obtain was the *Sufferings of the Friends in Cornwall*. We read harrowing accounts of Quakers being dragged over cobblestones and beaten with rods. I salute Ambrose, my distant ancestor, for the courage he showed all those years ago.

When I knew my grandmother Kitty she was living with a married daughter at Newland Hall in Essex. This was another ancient picturesque homestead. How well I remember the great pans of milk on the stove, waiting to be skimmed for Cornish cream. Later my brother owned this house and farmed several hundred acres of land; so for many years of my life before I married, it was the setting for holidays and week-end visits. We discovered much information about this house in *Morant's History of Essex*. This book we found in the Chelmsford County Library. Originally the house had been a hunting lodge for Harold the Saxon, who was defeated by William the Conqueror in 1066. Henry VIII too used Newland Hall as a retreat when he wanted to get away from affairs of state.

During World War II a landmine destroyed part of the building. An Elizabethan timbered front and many oak beams were uncovered before it was repaired. This house, unlike New Hall, was never a monastery. You will often find that the farmhouses of England contain a wealth of history within their walls. Newland Hall had a

secret passage now closed because it is unsafe. It led to a
copse some miles away, and could be used as an escape
route during times of seige.

In your County Reference Library you can find
various histories of counties. For instance *Clutterbuck's
History of Hertfordshire*, published in 1821, is in three
large volumes and contains not only accounts of villages,
parishes and houses, but many family trees. Such
County Histories are valuable for people who like delv-
ing into the past.

*   *   *

Writing a Family History: Paternal Grandmother

If your father's mother is still alive question her politely but in
great detail about her antecedents: her father and mother and her
grandparents. She may be able to carry you back quite a long
way.

It is possible that some members of her family lived in interesting houses, or were connected with historical movements, such as
the Suffragettes. Some of her male relations may have fought in
the First World War.

Making a Family Tree: Paternal Grandmother

Make a careful chart on your paternal grandmother's family, following the pattern already established, and join to father's chart at
the appropriate place.

References used in this chapter

The *Sufferings of the Friends in Cornwall*
Morant's *History of Essex*

My cousins in Cornwall have kept the various Family Bibles,
but I happen to possess a quaint Birthday Book belonging to my
late father's sister. Opposite each date in this faded little volume
there is a flower and a verse of poetry. One great-grandmother,
Rebecca Grose, wrote her date of birth as January 3rd, 1795,
which carries us back to the French Revolution.

5

FANFARE FOR ELEANOR: GREAT-GREAT-GRANDMOTHER

ALEXANDER MENHINICK, my great-great-great-grandfather was quite vexed when his daughter Elizabeth eloped with a poor carpenter, though later he forgave her. I wonder what he thought when his son John married a lady called Eleanor Cottell. This Eleanor was someone of higher rank than the farming Menhinicks. Without her I should not have been able to make such a long family tree. It is true that the Menhinicks could go back through ten generations to 1579, but Eleanor's family were able to link themselves to more than one royal line. She can go back so far that the traces are lost in the mists of antiquity.

The men in the Menhinick family would sign their names like this: Alexander Menhinick, yeoman; John Menhinick, yeoman. This meant that they were independent farmers, owning and tilling their own land. But Eleanor's father and grandfather could write even more proudly: Charles Cottell, gentleman; William Hocken, gentleman. This meant that they were landed gentry, either owning or connected with a large estate. They were upper-class, whereas the Menhinicks were middle-class. This may seem very snobbish to us now, but in the eighteenth century people in England had a clearly defined station in society; everyone knew his place.

How then do we account for the marriage of the yeoman with the gentleman's daughter? One reason may have been that in 1794, the year of his marriage to Eleanor, John Menhinick was living with his father at

Tregarden. This branch of the family usually employed governesses to teach the children and sometimes five maids indoors. Servants in an eighteenth century farmhouse would have been busy people; there would have been much baking of bread, yeast cake and Cornish pasties; there would have been churning butter and making cheese, even spinning and weaving in this remote countryside. Thus Eleanor would have been a person of some importance as mistress of a large household. We know too that the men from that side of the family were over six feet tall and quite handsome.

All the same I am filled with curiosity about Eleanor. No one remembers her, no one can describe her to me in detail; there is a strange silence. I have two teenage great-nephews, Kevin and Stephen Menhinick, and now I have a granddaughter called Helen Guinevere. To these youngsters I can give, in vivid word pictures, an account of Maggie and Kitty, their great-great-grandmothers. These ladies, however, lived to be quite old and their photographs could be taken. Poor Eleanor died at thirty in 1802, having borne five children in eight years. In her day photography had not been invented. My brother married at twenty-three and my nephew at twenty-five, but my father was over forty on his wedding day. Thus the lapse of time between myself and Eleanor is much greater. There are in fact one hundred and three years between her death and my birth. But we know that she was a real person and that I am her direct descendant. Much information about her came from the British Museum and the Genealogical Society in London.

It is interesting to notice that the Christian name Charles entered the Menhinick family through the Cottells. Before Eleanor arrived on the scene the chief male Christian names had been Alexander and John. There had however been three generations of Charles Cottells closely connected with Eleanor, so she gave this name to her new family. It was my father's name and it belonged to his uncle and grandfather. My brother, my son and a great-nephew all carry Charles as their second name. So the unknown, mysterious Eleanor can never be forgotten.

After the early death of Eleanor, the widower, John Menhinick, moved to Burniere, an attractive homestead near Wadebridge. Here still live his direct descendants, my second cousins, Ruth and John Menhinick. So the eldest son of the eldest son has occupied the same house and farmed the same land for over one hundred and seventy years.

With Eleanor's ancestors we begin to enter into English history. Her great-great-grandfather was Mark Cottell, a member of the Inner Temple, which means that he was an important lawyer. His wife Ursula Dobbins, was the daughter of Daniel Dobbins of Kidderminster, a member of parliament for Bewdley in Oliver Cromwell's much reduced, hastily summoned assembly known as the *Barebones Parliament*. No doubt your ancestors took part in the Civil War between the Roundheads and the Cavaliers in the seventeenth century. It seems here that at least one of my forbears was a Roundhead fighting on Cromwell's side against King Charles I.

Now if we go back six more generations we find that in the fifteenth century there was a John Cottell of Yealmbridge, on the borders of Devon and Cornwall, who married Margery Godfrey, daughter of Nicholas Godfrey. She brought a crest into the Cottell family.

A crest is a device or design from the age of chivalry which knights wore on their helmets or shields. Each knight was proud of his own family's crest. Marriage would sometimes bring in additional emblems so that one coat of arms would contain more than one device. Margery Godfrey brought the Cottells a design showing a black griffin on a silver field. A griffin is a fabulous mon-

ster half eagle and half lion; something from a fairy
story, not like any animal in the real world.

The study of crests and coats of arms is known as
heraldry. This study is distinct from genealogy (names
in a family) and there are many reference books on heraldry in public libraries.

The father of this John Cottell of Yealmbridge,
another John Cottell, is the head of this branch of the
pedigree (family tree) registered in the Herald's College,
and this John Cottell senior again links us to English
history in a very special way. He married a lady called
Sarah Carhurta, whose father was Roger Carhurta,
gentleman, of Devon. Note once more the use of the
word gentleman to describe his rank or status. Sarah's
father's mother was Margery Malherbe, and four generations back we come to Roger Malherbe, who in 1334
bought two hundred acres of land at Ottery St. Mary in
Devon.

This Roger Malherbe was directly descended from
the Malherbe whose name appears on the roll of Battle
Abbey. This means that he came over and fought side by
side with William the Conqueror in 1066. The Malherbe
pedigree was found by us in the *History of Trigg Minor*,
a book we obtained from the County Library in Truro.
An Abbey at Battle near Hastings was founded by William the Conqueror in thanksgiving for his victory. In
1966, nine hundred years after this famous date, a pa-
geant was held in the very field where the Normans and
Saxons fought each other. I drove down to watch it. University students engaged in a mock battle on opposing
sides. Little boys shouted encouragement: 'Go on
Harold; go on Harold'. Unfortunately history cannot be
rewritten. Harold fell and one of my ancestors was help-
ing in his defeat.

*　　　*　　　*

Writing a Family History: Great-great-grandmother

It is possible that your grandmother may be able to tell you about your great-great-grandmother who was *her* grandmother. People in the twentieth century are living longer and because of the invention of photography and sound recording we have more opportunity of definite contact with past generations. (For example Princess Anne can talk with living relatives who knew Queen Victoria, her great-great-great-grandmother, quite well. You could make a simple Tree showing the relationship of Princess Anne and Prince Charles to Queen Victoria.)

Your grandparents may have a collection of old photographs and other family documents, newspaper cuttings and mementos which could be incorporated into your history.

Making a Family Tree: Great-great-grandmother

This particular Tree concentrates on the one great-great grandmother, Eleanor Cottell, because she can be traced far back through several important families to Edward I who reigned from 1272–1307. You may only wish to trace your family back as far as your great-great grandparents or to the most important of your ancestors. Whatever its length your Tree, with your illustrated Family History, will make fascinating reading for all your relatives. It will be an even more valuable study for your descendants.

At this stage all your charts can be combined and even re-drawn to make a completely branching Tree. If properly finished this could be a decorative feature in your home.

Your ancestors, whoever they were, made their contribution to life as we know it today, by their work, by their inventions, by their sufferings and by their sacrifices. Everyone has his place in history.

References used in this chapter

History of Trigg Minor by Sir John Maclean (3 volumes, 1873)
Ancient West Country Families and their Armorial Bearings by Williams, 1916
The *Encyclopedia Britannica*

Chart 5B

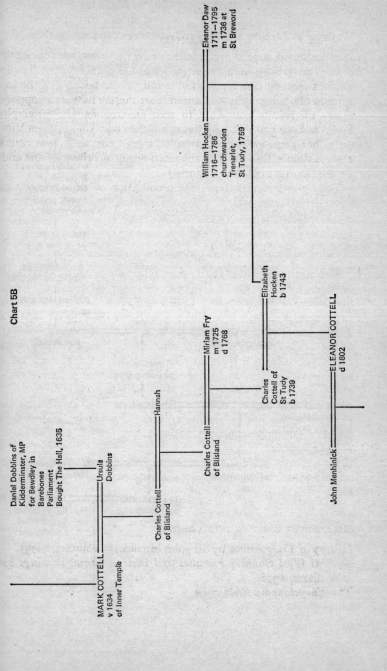

Daniel Dobbins of
Kidderminster, MP
for Bewdley in
Barebones
Parliament
Bought The Hall, 1635

Eleanor Daw
1711–1795
m 1736 at
St Breword

William Hocken
1716–1786
churchwarden
Trenarlet,
St Tudy, 1759

MARK COTTELL
v 1634
of Inner Temple

Ursula
Dobbins

Charles Cottell
of Blisland

Hannah

Charles Cottell
of Blisland

Miriam Fry
m 1725
d 1768

Elizabeth
Hocken
b 1743

Charles
Cottell of
St Tudy
b 1739

John Menhinick

ELEANOR COTTELL
d 1802

Chart 5D

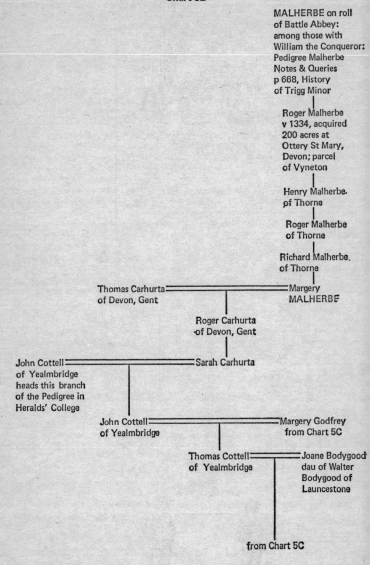

MALHERBE on roll
of Battle Abbey:
among those with
William the Conqueror:
Pedigree Malherbe
Notes & Queries
p 668, History
of Trigg Minor

Roger Malherbe
v 1334, acquired
200 acres at
Ottery St Mary,
Devon; parcel
of Vyneton

Henry Malherbe.
of Thorne

Roger Malherbe
of Thorne

Richard Malherbe.
of Thorne

Thomas Carhurta ═══════════════ Margery
of Devon, Gent   MALHERBE

Roger Carhurta
of Devon, Gent

John Cottell ═══════════════ Sarah Carhurta
of Yealmbridge
heads this branch
of the Pedigree in
Heralds' College

John Cottell ═══════════════ Margery Godfrey
of Yealmbridge   from Chart 5C

Thomas Cottell ═══════════════ Joane Bodygood
of Yealmbridge   dau of Walter
                               Bodygood of
                               Launcestone

from Chart 5C

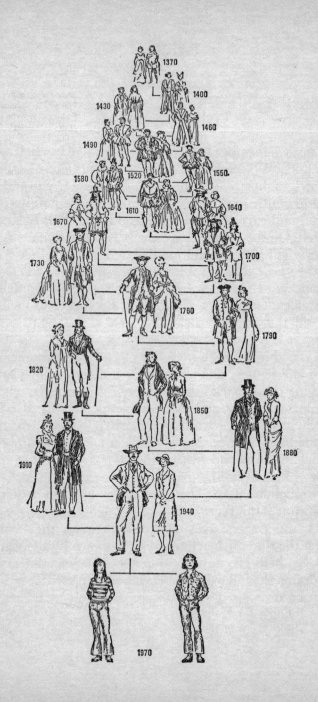

PART II

Preface to Part II

We must remember that everyone has a great choice of ancestors. We have all had two parents, four grandparents, eight great-grandparents, sixteen great-great-grandparents. In this way the branches of a family tree spread and carry us backwards. So it was with Eleanor Cottell. On the female side especially she had many forbears who led quite exciting lives. So in Part II we will now see how through marriage she became related to famous West Country families such as the Arundells, Grenvilles, Courtneys and the de Bohuns. She finally entered the English royal line in the thirteenth century.

It was through such marriages that we find more and more key figures, linking with even older families and carrying us far back into the past. In those days, when people had many children, the branches spread ever more widely, for these children married in their turn and founded new homes. As we make our journey through time we shall see how these ancestors are linked to the story of Britain itself.

Throughout Part II Charts are used in tracing significant families, marriages, high offices, large properties and estates. Key figures appear on the chart. Along the side of the charts time is shown by the years A.D. To help give information about the characters in the drama the following abbreviations are used:

b   born
v   living
d   died

r   reigned
c   about
dau daughter
m   married
(i)   1st wife or 1st husband
(2)   2nd wife or 2nd husband
Names related to royal lines are shown thus

SIX SWALLOWS AND A SCOTTISH PIRATE

THE Mark Cottell of the Inner Temple whom we met in Chapter 5 had a mother whose maiden name was Mary Cosworth. There is not much of interest to say about the Cosworths, who can be traced back to 1420, except to notice that Mary's grandfather, John Cosworth, left behind a brass monument in Colan church,

about three miles from Newquay. These brasses are portraits of well-known people etched on the floors of churches. It is a popular and absorbing hobby to take brass rubbings. Put a large piece of plain paper over the brass and rub it all over with heel black. Permission from the local vicar must first be obtained. In many cases a small charge is made.

Mary Cosworth's mother was Dorothy Arundell. The Arundells were a very important West Country family. The name itself comes from *hirondelle*, the French for swallow, and indeed the shield of the family contains six swallows.

In the Middle Ages surnames came into fashion because it was confusing to have so many Williams and Johns. Names were given according to trade or profession. If your name is Smith your ancestors may have been workers in copper or bronze. If it is Fletcher then they may have fixed feathers to arrows. The name Ford means that your forbears lived near a ford; the name Redhead explains itself. The Menhinicks simply took over a place name: Menegby Nyot. The Davidsons and Andersons, being originally from Scandinavia, followed the Viking custom of calling a man, son of David or son of Andrew. Later the name Arundell became corrupted and today often appears as Rundell or Randall.

The earliest Cornish Arundell we could find was Roger de Arundell who held manors in Devon and Cornwall and who is mentioned in the Domesday Book. This was a survey ordered by William the Conqueror in 1086 to find out the exact ownership of land throughout the kingdom. After the Conquest much of the land had been taken from the English thegns or nobles and given to the Normans. William was anxious to discover who possessed the various estates so that the correct taxes could be paid to the Crown. The survey was searching and thorough; even the teams of oxen and the fisheries were included. Very few Cornish families are of Norman origin; that south-west corner was isolated from the rest of the country, but the Arundells came from Normandy as their French name reveals.

Coming forward in time we find an unusual entry. In

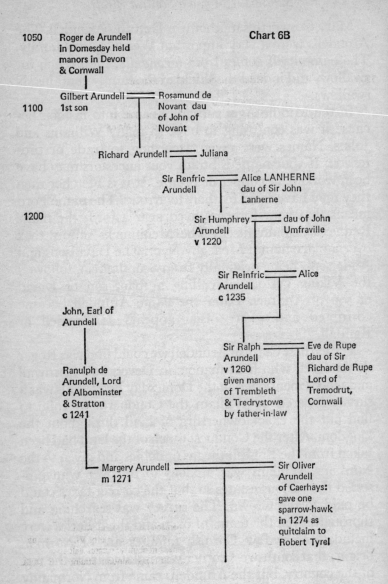

1050   Roger de Arundell
In Domesday held
manors in Devon
& Cornwall

Chart 6B

Gilbert Arundell ===== Rosamund de
1100   1st son   Novant dau
                        of John of
                        Novant

Richard Arundell ===== Juliana

Sir Renfric ===== Alice LANHERNE
Arundell   dau of Sir John
                  Lanherne

1200

Sir Humphrey ===== dau of John
Arundell   Umfraville
v 1220

Sir Reinfric ===== Alice
Arundell
c 1235

John, Earl of
Arundell

Sir Ralph ===== Eve de Rupe
Arundell   dau of Sir
v 1260   Richard de Rupe
given manors   Lord of
Ranulph de   of Trembleth   Tremodrut,
Arundell, Lord   & Tredrystowe   Cornwall
of Albominster   by father-in-law
& Stratton
c 1241

Margery Arundell ============ Sir Oliver
m 1271   Arundell
                                  of Caerhays:
                                  gave one
                                  sparrow-hawk
                                  in 1274 as
                                  quitclaim to
                                  Robert Tyrel

1300

Ralph-Arundell ═══ Elizabeth
of Caerhays   Seneschal dau
in 1303 sued   of Sir John
Roger de   Seneschal, Kt
Ingepinne for   Lord of Manor
breaking,   of Trerice
entering &
stealing from
coffers, cups
.of silver
worth 10/-
& 40/-

to Chart 6C

Trerice Arundells
had coat-of-arms
differing from
Lanherne, but
finally both
branches had the
6 swallows

3 main Arundell lines: LANHERNE
(oldest), TRERICE, TOLVERNE.
Lanherne branch styled 'the great
Arundell s'settled in Cornwall mid-
13th C or earlier at Trembleath.
Roger Arundell (Lanherne) was
Marshall of England: William,
d 1246, canon of Exeter Cathedral.
Arundells married with old and
'important Cornish families:
Carminow, Grenville, Beville,
Lambourne, Carew, Trevanion,
Erisy. TRERICE Arundells had
seats in Newlyn parish 5 miles from
Langherne & parts of 16th C
mansion remain. John Arundell
by 1421, time of Henry VI, largest free
tenant in county: estates valued at
2,000 1. per annum: attainted' in 1483.

1274 Sir Oliver Arundell of Caerhays gave one sparrow-hawk to Sir Robert Tyrel in 'quit claim'. Evidently Oliver owed something to Robert or had offended him in some way so he gave him a sparrow-hawk to settle the matter.

In 1370 Oliver's great grandson Nicholas was 'abducted while a minor'. This means that he was kidnapped and probably held to ransom. He must have been rescued for he married and continued the Arundell line.

Nicholas' son, Sir John Arundell, became known as the Magnificent. He was a great benefactor to the church, notably the lost church of St. Piran-in-the-Sands, a building since swallowed up by the sea. His Will in 1433 listed fifty-two suits of cloth of gold. Evidently some men in those days liked to look smart. In his Will he also left forty shillings to 'enclose suitably the head of St. Piran'. St. Piran was an Irish saint who long ago was supposed to have crossed the sea to England riding on a millstone. It was important to have a casket which would hold such a sacred object, the head of this holy man. In the Middle Ages people set great store by the relics or bodily remains of saints long since dead and often attributed miracles of healing to their power. This Sir John was a naval commander and Sheriff of Cornwall four times. In 1422 he became a Member of Parliament. By now the Arundells were the most powerful landowners in Cornwall, having gained added territory through wealthy marriages. This family is quite distinct from the Sussex Arundells who now hold Arundell Castle.

The grandson of this last-mentioned gentleman was yet another Sir John, who became a vice-admiral. He was sent by Edward IV to take St. Michael's Mount, which had been seized by the Earl of Oxford. A prophecy from a chronicle had foretold that he would be 'slain in the sands', so to avoid this fate he moved inland to the manor of Trerice, which is still a stately home today. However he met his death on the sands of St. Michael's Mount in 1471. His remains are in the church there; thus his precautions were of no avail.

The grandson or great-nephew of this Sir John was yet another Sir John Arundell (1494–1561). He was appointed by Henry VIII as an esquire of the body, a sort of royal bodyguard. He was a vice-admiral of the Fleet and became known as *Jack of Tilbury*. In 1523, after a long sea-battle, he captured a notorious Scottish pirate, Duncan Campbell, who had 'long scourged our coasts'. He was asked to bring this dangerous man in chains to the king's presence.

Jack of Tilbury's wife, Julia Erisy, a lady from another powerful Cornish family, with two royal connections, links us to English history in an exciting way.

Chart 6C

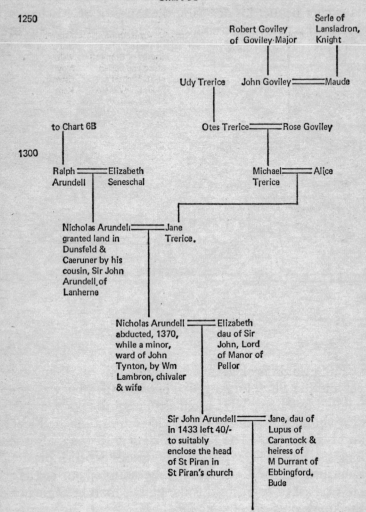

1250

Robert Goviley
of Goviley-Major

Serle of
Lansladron,
Knight

Udy Trerice

John Goviley════════Maude

to Chart 6B

Otes Trerice════════Rose Goviley

1300

Ralph════════Elizabeth
Arundell   Seneschal

Michael════════Alice
Trerice

Nicholas Arundell════════Jane
granted land in   Trerice.
Dunsfeld &
Caeruner by his
cousin, Sir John
Arundell of
Lanherne

Nicholas Arundell════════Elizabeth
abducted, 1370,   dau of Sir
while a minor,   John, Lord
ward of John   of Manor of
Tynton, by Wm   Pellor
Lambron, chivaler
& wife

Sir John Arundell════════Jane, dau of
in 1433 left 40/-   Lupus of
to suitably   Carantock &
enclose the head   heiress of
of St Piran in   M Durrant of
St Piran's church   Ebbingford,
                             Bude

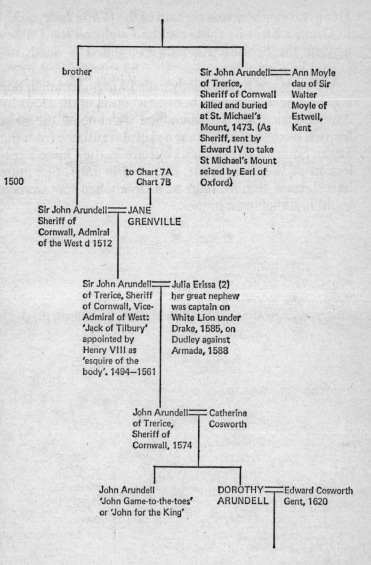

brother

Sir John Arundell
of Trerice,
Sheriff of Cornwall
killed and buried
at St. Michael's
Mount, 1473. (As
Sheriff, sent by
Edward IV to take
St Michael's Mount
seized by Earl of
Oxford)══Ann Moyle
dau of Sir
Walter
Moyle of
Estwell,
Kent

to Chart 7A
Chart 7B

1500

Sir John Arundell══JANE
Sheriff of   GRENVILLE
Cornwall, Admiral
of the West d 1512

Sir John Arundell══Julia Erissa (2)
of Trerice, Sheriff her great nephew
of Cornwall, Vice- was captain on
Admiral of West: White Lion under
'Jack of Tilbury'   Drake, 1585, on
appointed by   Dudley against
Henry VIII as   Armada, 1588
'esquire of the
body'. 1494—1561

John Arundell══Catherine
of Trerice,   Cosworth
Sheriff of
Cornwall, 1574

John Arundell
'John Game-to-the-toes'
or 'John for the King'

DOROTHY══Edward Cosworth
ARUNDELL   Gent, 1620

Her great-nephew was captain of the *White Lion*, a ship in Drake's Fleet in 1585, and he fought on the *Dudley* against the Spanish Armada in 1588. His death occurred in 1601.

We must not forget a lady called Mary Arundell. She is not a direct ancestress but was a cousin of the Dorothy Arundell mentioned earlier. She was one of the most learnéd women of her time: a skilful translator from the Latin. Some of her manuscripts are in the Queen's collection at Windsor Castle. She died in 1691. She must have been a shining light at a time when few women could sign their own names.

*   *   *

References:
Dictionary of National Biography
Encyclopedia Britannica
History of Trigg Minor by Sir John Maclean (3 volumes, 1873)

7

ENTERING THE ROYAL LINE

Jane Grenville (1500)

ANOTHER interesting Cornish family were the Grenvilles of Stowe. Nowadays their name appears in varying forms: Granville, Grenfell, even Greenfield. I am linked to them through Jack of Tilbury's mother, who was Jane Grenville before she became Jane Arundell. Eleven 'greats' before the title of grandmother gives the exact relationship. A study of the chart 7a shows how her collaterals or side-shoots fit into English history.

Jane's great-great-nephew was Sir Richard Grenville, a famous seaman and a cousin of Sir Walter Raleigh, the poet and explorer. Sir Richard was a proud, ambitious man of great courage. At an early age he served in Hungary under the Emperor Maximilian, fighting the Turkish invaders. In 1591 Grenville was appointed

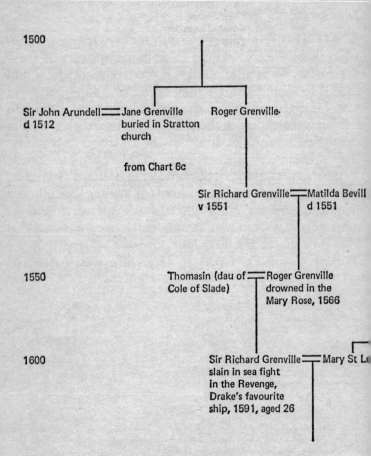

1500

Sir John Arundell══Jane Grenville
d 1512   buried in Stratton
                     church

Roger Grenville·

from Chart 6c

Sir Richard Grenville══Matilda Bevill
v 1551   d 1551

1550

Thomasin (dau of══Roger Grenville
Cole of Slade)   drowned in the
                    Mary Rose, 1566

1600

Sir Richard Grenville══Mary St Le
slain in sea fight
in the Revenge,
Drake's favourite
ship, 1591, aged 26

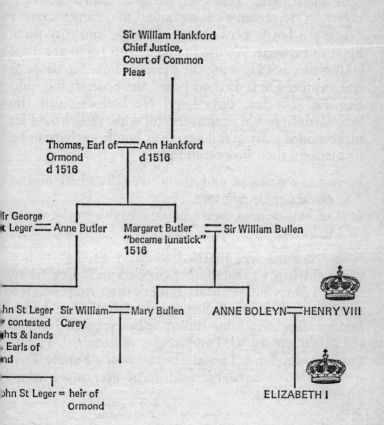

Sir William Hankford
Chief Justice,
Court of Common
Pleas

Thomas, Earl of ═══ Ann Hankford
Ormond   d 1516
d 1516

Sir George
St Leger ═══ Anne Butler   Margaret Butler ═══ Sir William Bullen
                                 "became lunatick"
                                 1516

John St Leger   Sir William ═══ Mary Bullen   ANNE BOLEYN ═══ HENRY VIII
contested   Carey
rights & lands
of Earls of
Ormond

John St Leger = heir of
               Ormond

                                                    ELIZABETH I

second in command on board the *Revenge*, a ship which had been commanded by Drake in 1588 against the Spanish Armada. Tennyson, the great nineteenth century poet, wrote an exciting ballad to commemorate a heroic sea battle between the *Revenge* and fifty-three Spanish galleons. We used to recite this poem at school with gusto, not knowing the personal link. Sir Richard was captured and died on board the Spanish flag-ship *San Pablo* a few days later. He had engaged the Spaniards in battle against fearful odds, rather than let his wounded seamen fall into their hands, perhaps to be tortured for their Protestant Faith:

For some were sunk and many were shattered, and so
    could fight us no more.
God of battles, was ever a battle like this in the world
    before?

Sir Richard was married to Mary St. Leger. See Chart 7(a) Mary's grandfather, Sir George St. Leger, had married Mary Butler. Mary Butler's sister Anne was the wife of Sir William Bullen. Anne and William had a famous daughter, Anne Bullen or Boleyn, who became the wife of Henry VIII and mother of Elizabeth Tudor, Queen of England. Thus the branches of a Family Tree spread always outwards and form ever more complicated patterns.

Margaret Courtenay

Jane Grenville leads us directly backwards as well as forwards. Jane's great-great-grandfather, Theobald Grenville, married a lady called Margaret Courtenay in 1390. The Courtenay family itself has an ancient and complicated history. In 1010 a Frenchman named Athon fortified the town of Courtenay which lay about a hundred miles south of Paris, and then took the name of that town for his own surname. His great-great-granddaughter Elizabeth married into the French royal house, becoming the wife of Prince Pierre, the seventh son of King Louis VI, who was nicknamed the Fat. Pierre decided to take his wife's name, so his descendants were known as de Courtenays.

When Louis the Fat's eldest son became Louis VII the Courtenay relatives were treated shabbily. The new king seized their French possessions and drove two brothers, Reginald and Robert Courtenay, into exile. These young men came to England in the twelfth century to seek their fortune and soon became linked with stirring events in English history. Robert married the daughter of Reinhold FitzUrze, leader of the four knights who murdered Thomas a Becket in Canterbury Cathedral. Reginald found favour with King Henry II and accompanied him on his Irish expedition of 1172. Henry gave him *Sutton Courtenay* in Berkshire in 1161; this place is still on the map. The Courtenays married into powerful English and French families, such as the Vernons, the Clares, and even the descendants of William the Conqueror. By this means they acquired castles and large estates and became earls of Devon.

William Courtenay (1342–1396) became Archbishop of Canterbury in 1381 and performed the wedding ceremony between Richard II and Anne of Bohemia. He publicly rebuked the king for his extravagance. Certainly Richard dressed in a flamboyant style, with elaborate sleeves and pointed shoes. The shoes were copied from the up-curving slippers of the Saracens, a fashion brought back from the Crusades. The toes were so elongated that they had to be caught by jewelled chains to garters just below the knee.

Because of this open criticism of his royal master

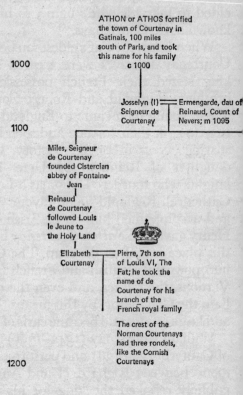

ATHON or ATHOS fortified
the town of Courtenay in
Gatinais, 100 miles
south of Paris, and took
this name for his family
c 1000

1000

Josselyn (I) ═══ Ermengarde, dau of
Seigneur de   Reinaud, Count of
Courtenay   Nevers; m 1095

1100

Miles, Seigneur
de Courtenay
founded Cistercian
abbey of Fontaine-
Jean

Reinaud
de Courtenay
followed Louis
le Jeune to
the Holy Land

Elizabeth ═══ Pierre, 7th son
Courtenay   of Louis VI, The
                 Fat; he took the
                 name of de
                 Courtenay for his
                 branch of the
                 French royal family

The crest of the
Norman Courtenays
had three rondels,
like the Cornish
Courtenays

1200

Chart 7C

Robert (I)
younger son

King Louis VII took Norman lands
from Courtenays, so Robert and
Reginald came to England

Robert de Courtenay
n dau of Reinhold
itzUrze, leader of
e 4 knights who
illed Becket at
Canterbury

Reginald (I)
de Courtenay
favourite of
Henry II of
England; with
King on Irish
expedition.
King gave him Sutton
Courtenay in Berkshire
1161

1st wife in Normandy
2nd wife Maude Fitzroy
descended from William
the Conqueror's niece

to Chart 7D

Archbishop William had to leave the court and retire to Devonshire, but he was later recalled. On one occasion the king's uncle, John of Gaunt, was so angry with the Archbishop that he threatened to drag him from St. Paul's Cathedral by his hair. The people of London came to his defence so poor William was saved from the indignity of having his hair torn out.

Margaret de Bohun

The next key figure in the family is Margaret de Bohun, who was the great-great-grandmother of Margaret Courtenay. Margaret de Bohun, at the tender age of thirteen, married Hugh de Courtenay, second earl of Devon, who drove back the French attack on Cornwall in 1339 and is buried in Exeter Cathedral. One of her sons was the Archbishop William Courtenay who dared to find fault with Richard II. Her grandson Edward, Earl Marshall

Chart 7D

from Chart 7C

1150

1200

1300

1400

Reginald (I)══════1st wife in
de Courtenay   France

de Veres descended from
Albericus (Aubrey) v 1086
in Domesday held fiefs in
Essex, Cambridge, Suffolk.
Name from village of Ver
near Bayeux

Reginald (II)══════Hawise
de Courtenay   d'Ayencourt
m by 1178   heiress of
                    Okehampton

Robert (III)══════Mary de Vernon
de Courtenay   younger dau of
succeeded to   William de Vernon,
Okehampton 1219   Earl of Devon
& Sutton from   & Isle of Wight
his uncle 1209

John de Courtenay══════Isabel de Vere
succeeded to   dau of Hugh
Okehampton 1242,   de Vere, 6th
Constable of   Earl of Oxford
Castle of Totnes.

Eleanor Le Despenser's
mother was Eleanor de
Clare, dau of The Red
Earl, Gilbert de Clare,
Earl of Gloucester;
most powerful subject
in the land, killed at
Bannockburn. De Clares
descended from de Brionne
who m. Albriaa, niece of
William the Conqueror

Hugh (II) de══════Eleanor Le
Courtenay   Despenser
1250–1291

Hugh (III)══════Agnes
de Courtenay   dau of
Baron of   Lord St John
Okehampton,
Admiral of
West Seas
d 1340

MARGARET DE BOHUN══════Hugh (IV) de
1312–1391   Courtenay, 2nd
m 1325!   Earl of Devon;
                        d 1377. Repulsed
                        attack on Cornwall
                        1339. Buried in
                        Exeter Cathedral

to Chart 7E

of England, was known as the Blind Earl, and his heir, either a son or a nephew, was one of the heroes of Agincourt (1415) when Henry V was victorious over the French, though their army was three times the size of the English force. Shakespeare's exciting play *Henry V* tells of these events. The name Bohun came from a village in north-west France, not far from the island of Jersey. The de Bohuns came to England soon after the Norman Conquest. The third Humfry de Bohun was appointed steward in Henry I's household and from this time the family rose in Wealth and importance.

The de Bohun Family

The most frequent male name of the de Bohuns was Humfry. When such a name is given generation after generation among men who are not of royal blood the numeral is put in parentheses: Humfry (I), Humfry (II) etc. The kings are shown simply as Edward I or Edward II. The first de Bohun was Humfry 'with the Beard' (c 1066) and his son, Humfry (II) was captured in a battle at Winchester in 1141. Both Humfry (IV) c 1199, and Humfry (V) c 1239, married ladies descended from the royal house of Scotland. Humfry (IV) married Margaret, daughter of Prince Henry of Scotland, and Humfry (V) married Maud Hastings, Prince Henry's great-granddaughter.

The most significant of the Humfrys was Margaret de Bohun's father, Humfry (VIII) 1284–1321. He went with the weak Edward II to fight the Scots and was captured at the famous Battle of Bannockburn in 1314. The skilful and courageous Scottish troops defeated the English, who were four times as numerous, in an overwhelming victory, thus ensuring Scotland's independence for centuries. However Humfry was ex-

Chart 7F

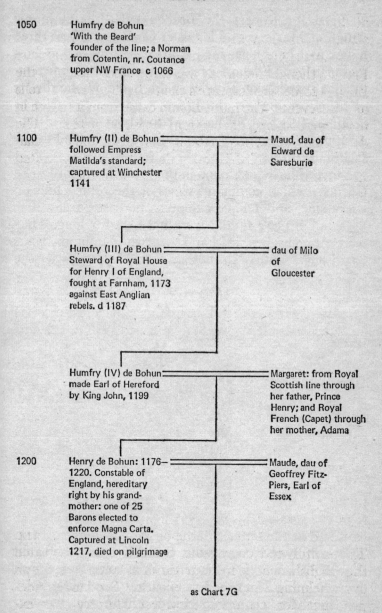

1050   Humfry de Bohun
'With the Beard'
founder of the line; a Norman
from Cotentin, nr. Coutance
upper NW France **c 1066**

1100   Humfry (II) de Bohun   Maud, dau of
followed Empress   Edward de
Matilda's standard;   Saresburie
captured at Winchester
1141

        Humfry (III) de Bohun   dau of Milo
Steward of Royal House   of
for Henry I of England,   Gloucester
fought at Farnham, 1173
against East Anglian
rebels. d 1187

        Humfry (IV) de Bohun   Margaret: from Royal
made Earl of Hereford   Scottish line through
by King John, 1199   her father, Prince
                                      Henry; and Royal
                                      French (Capet) through
                                      her mother, Adama

1200   Henry de Bohun: 1176–   Maude, dau of
1220. Constable of   Geoffrey Fitz-
England, hereditary   Piers, Earl of
right by his grand-   Essex
mother: one of 25
Barons elected to
enforce Magna Carta.
Captured at Lincoln
1217, died on pilgrimage

                    as Chart 7G

changed for Robert the Bruce's wife Elizabeth, his daughter Marjory, and his sister Christian. These three ladies had long been held captive in England as hostages. In 1307 Edward I had captured these women on his final expedition to subdue the Scots, for he died a month later. Robert the Bruce, who was Robert I of Scotland (1274–1329) had sent them for safety to Kildrummie Castle in Aberdeenshire, while he fled to the Island of Rathlin.

I myself have had lunch in the beautiful Kildrummie Gardens which command views of the rolling hills on every side, and I have explored the castle ruins. The ladies of Bruce's family were not safe for long. They were seized by Edward I and spent seven unhappy years as prisoners south of the border. Poor Marjory, when she

was only twelve, was hung up in a cage outside the Tower of London, to endure bitter cold, hunger and homesickness. Later she was allowed to join her mother, who had been kept a prisoner in another castle.

Chart 7G

from Chart 7F

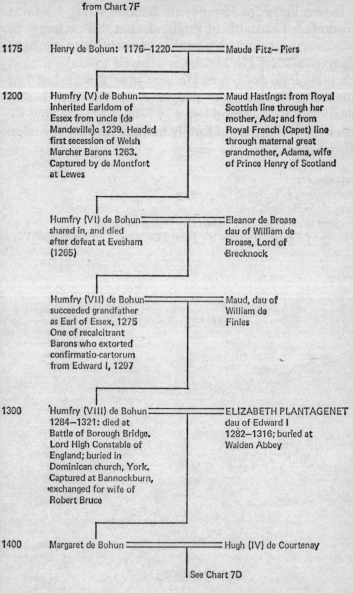

1175 Henry de Bohun: 1176–1220 ════ Maude Fitz—Piers

1200 Humfry (V) de Bohun ════ Maud Hastings: from Royal
inherited Earldom of Scottish line through her
Essex from uncle (de mother, Ada; and from
Mandeville)c 1239. Headed Royal French (Capet) line
first secession of Welsh through maternal great
Marcher Barons 1263. grandmother, Adama, wife
Captured by de Montfort of Prince Henry of Scotland
at Lewes

Humfry (VI) de Bohun ════ Eleanor de Broase
shared in, and died dau of William de
after defeat at Evesham Broase, Lord of
(1265) Brecknock

Humfry (VII) de Bohun ════ Maud, dau of
succeeded grandfather William de
as Earl of Essex, 1275 Finles
One of recalcitrant
Barons who extorted
confirmatio-cartorum
from Edward I, 1297

1300 Humfry (VIII) de Bohun ════ ELIZABETH PLANTAGENET
1284–1321: died at dau of Edward I
Battle of Borough Bridge. 1282–1316; buried at
Lord High Constable of Walden Abbey
England; buried in
Dominican church, York.
Captured at Bannockburn,
exchanged for wife of
Robert Bruce

1400 Margaret de Bohun ════ Hugh (IV) de Courtenay

See Chart 7D

T–C

It was lucky for Humfry de Bohun (VIII), who was Lord High Constable of England, that this exchange of prisoners went through and that he was able to return to his native land. He had been allowed to make a most advantageous marriage. He was now the husband of Elizabeth Plantagenet, daughter of Edward I and Eleanor of Castile, and sister of Edward II. So now we enter the English royal family and are directly linked to King Edward I.

References:
Dictionary of National Biography
Encyclopedia Britannica
Ancient West Country Families by Williams, 1916
History of Trigg Minor by Sir John Maclean (3 volumes, 1873)

8

MARGARET OF SCOTLAND

IF you study carefully the royal Family Trees of England, Scotland and Normandy (the province in France from which William the Conqueror came) you will find so many intermarriages, so many alliances, that it is almost as though someone gave you a master key. Once you establish a link with a royal line you can open any door you wish and there on the threshold will be an aunt or a cousin to welcome you.

Humfry de Bohun (VIII) was descended from Malcolm III of Scotland, who was nicknamed Canmore or Bighead. Sometimes we call conceited people that, but in this case it just meant that his head was large. Again King Edward I, another direct ancestor was also descended from Malcolm, because his great-great- great-grandfather, Henry I, had married Eadgyth, daughter of that same Scottish king. Alliances with Scotland were especially valuable to heal the wounds caused by the incessant fighting between the two countries. Now Malcolm III of Scotland had a lovely and talented Queen, later known as St. Margaret (1045–1093). Although removed by nine hundred years, this lady can be proudly claimed as an ancestress.

Margaret of Scotland had been an Anglo-Saxon princess, the daughter of Edward the Exile, and granddaughter of Edmund Ironside. Her father and her uncle had been sent by the Danish King Canute to Poland with a hint that he would be grateful if they never returned. Canute feared that they would threaten his position on the English throne when they grew up. The King of Poland did not wish to stain his hands with murder so he sent the little princes on to relatives in Hungary. Later, when one of them married, Margaret was born in that country. She and her brother, Edgar the Aethling (prince of the Saxon line) came to take refuge in Scotland because by now William the Conqueror was master of England. Malcolm King of Scotland began to woo Margaret. At first she refused his courtship because she wanted to dedicate her life to God, but when her brother agreed to the proposal, she finally yielded. This arranged marriage seems to have been a very happy one.

Margaret loved beauty in all its forms. She invited foreign merchants to bring richly embroidered garments for the Scottish courtiers to wear. She taught the Scottish ladies how to do this embroidery themselves. She introduced goblets and dishes of silver and gold for the nobles to use at table, and persuaded them to eat their food in a more elegant fashion. Remember that at this time Scotland was a wild backward country, remote from the rest of Europe. Margaret did much to introduce the civilized customs she had known in Hungary into this northern kingdom.

This Queen was a deeply religious woman. She rebuilt the monastery of Iona, the sacred island where Scottish kings were buried. Her room was like a 'workshop of celestial art' adorned with copes and altar cloths for the priests to use. The monk Turgot, who knew her well and who wrote her life-story in his chronicle in 1100 A.D., recalls that the people 'loved her with fear, and feared her with love'. She was a learned woman and had a 'Great greed for holy volumes'. Her husband, Malcolm Canmore, could not read, but often gazed at her books with tenderness and reverence; sometimes he would give orders that these mysterious volumes should be covered with precious jewels, just to give her pleasure. You may well ask why he did not learn to read himself, but in those days kings were men of action, leaving book-learning to monks and priests, or more rarely to women.

A charming story has come down concerning Margaret's bejewelled Book of the Gospels. It fell into a river while she was travelling, but it was rescued unharmed. This same priceless volume may still be seen in the Bodleian Library at Oxford. Margaret brought about many reforms in Scotland's mode of worship. She introduced the celebration of Holy Communion on Easter Day and begged the people to do no manual work on Sundays.

Above all Queen Margaret loved to help the poor. Following Christ's example she washed their feet in public, showing great humility in spite of her high-rank. Twenty-four poor persons always accompanied her wherever she went. Sometimes she took garments from her own attendants to give to beggars. Sometimes she 'stole' golden coins from her husband to help those in need. One story is very touching. Every day nine baby orphans were brought in and placed on her knee to be fed with 'soft foods in which the age of babyhood delights'. Margaret would not have been interested in food values:

Chart 8a

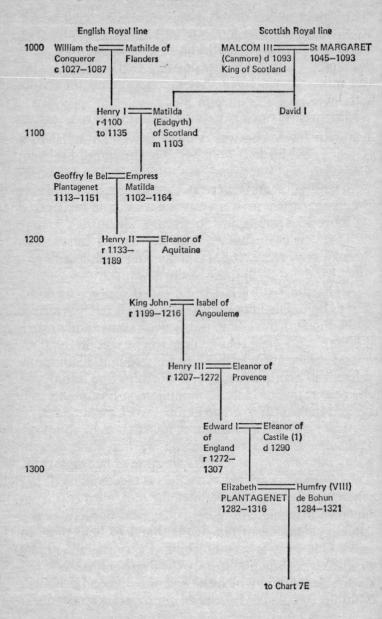

English Royal line | Scottish Royal line

1000   William the —— Mathilde of   MALCOM III ——St MARGARET
Conqueror   Flanders   (Canmore) d 1093   1045—1093
c 1027—1087   King of Scotland

Henry I —— Matilda   David I
r 1100   (Eadgyth)
1100   to 1135   of Scotland
m 1103

Geoffry le Bel —— Empress
Plantagenet   Matilda
1113—1151   1102—1164

1200   Henry II —— Eleanor of
r 1133—   Aquitaine
1189

King John —— Isabel of
r 1199—1216   Angouleme

Henry III —— Eleanor of
r 1207—1272   Provence

Edward I —— Eleanor of
of   Castile (1)
England   d 1290
1300   r 1272—
1307

Elizabeth —— Humfry (VIII)
PLANTAGENET   de Bohun
1282—1316   1284—1321

to Chart 7E

the proteins and minerals, the vitamins A or C, which are such a feature of modern baby foods, specially prepared in tins or jars, would have been unknown to her. Perhaps she gave the babies porridge, perhaps just bread and milk, but we know that she performed these acts with love.

Margaret was kind to prisoners of war and to all slaves and captives. She would seek them out and beg her husband for their release. It is unlikely that he could refuse her anything. She also built guest-houses for the comfort of pilgrims on either side the Firth of Forth. The name of *Queensferry* has lasted to this day.

Malcolm was killed in battle while invading Northumbria. Without being told his wife guessed that he was dead. Her grief was so great that she herself died soon after. When her remains were taken from the castle,

which happened to be under siege, the departure was said to be 'hidden by a magic mist'. As her coffin was carried past her husband's grave it grew so heavy that no one could lift it, so they exhumed Malcolm's body and they were buried together at Dumfermline where their wedding ceremony had taken place. Margaret's head,

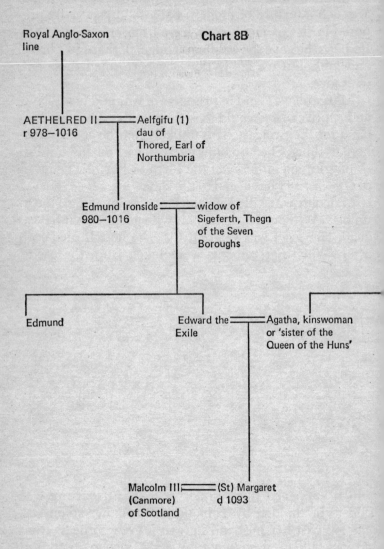

Royal Anglo-Saxon
line

AETHELRED II ════ Aelfgifu (1)
r 978–1016   dau of
                    Thored, Earl of
                    Northumbria

Edmund Ironside ════ widow of
980–1016   Sigeferth, Thegn
                      of the Seven
                      Boroughs

Edmund

Edward the ════ Agatha, kinswoman
Exile   or 'sister of the
                Queen of the Huns'

Malcolm III ════ (St) Margaret
(Canmore)   d 1093
of Scotland

MARGARET OF SCOTLAND
(her Anglo-Saxon,
Northumbrian,
Hungarian & Bavarian
origins)

Emperor Henry
The Quarrelsome
of Bavaria

a═══ (St) Stephen, King
of Hungary

Emperor
Henry II

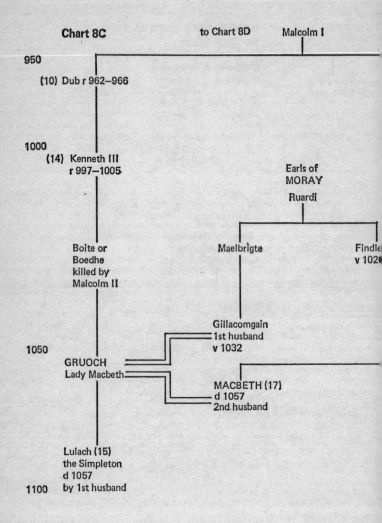

Chart 8C   to Chart 8D   Malcolm I

950

(10) Dub r 962–966

1000

(14) Kenneth III
r 997–1005

Earls of
MORAY

Ruardi

Boite or
Boedhe
killed by
Malcolm II

Maelbrigte

Findle
v 102

Gillacomgain
1st husband
v 1032

1050

GRUOCH
Lady Macbeth

MACBETH (17)
d 1057
2nd husband

Lulach (15)
the Simpleton
d 1057
1100   by 1st husband

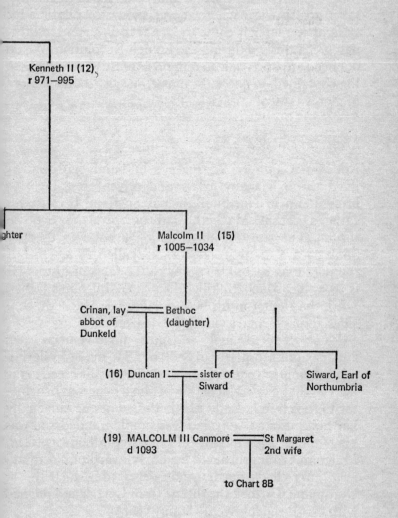

Kenneth II (12)
r 971–995

...ghter

Malcolm II (15)
r 1005–1034

Crinan, lay ⟹ Bethoc
abbot of   (daughter)
Dunkeld

(16) Duncan I ⟹ sister of   Siward, Earl of
                 Siward   Northumbria

(19) MALCOLM III Canmore ⟹ St Margaret
     d 1093   2nd wife

to Chart 8B

severed from her body, underwent strange adventures. Mary Queen of Scots at one time possessed it, then it was taken to Antwerp where it was shown to pilgrims for veneration; later it came to Douai in France. Unfortunately it vanished during the French Revolution. We do not need any such relic to remind us of this woman whose life contained, to quote the monk Turgot, 'so much more of mercy than of miracle'.

Malcolm and Macbeth

Malcolm Canmore, Margaret's husband, had himself lived through many trials and adventures. He was brought up in Northumbria not Scotland because his father's cousin Macbeth had usurped the Scottish throne. The story of this exciting event was used by Shakespeare in his tragic drama called *Macbeth* but the poet took some liberties with the facts of history. It is true that Macbeth killed Duncan, Malcolm's father, but in battle not in his bed, because he, Macbeth, considered that he had a claim to the throne.

Macbeth ruled wisely and justly for seventeen years and brought prosperity to Scotland. He made a pilgrimage to Rome in 1050 and 'scattered money like seed to the poor in that city'. Macbeth was also a generous benefactor to the church. Lady Macbeth had a son, Lulach, by her first husband. This lad was simple-minded and was king for only a few months, after his stepfather was killed. Malcolm Canmore, aided by Earl Siward of Northumbria, marched north and defeated Macbeth at Dunsinane. He took the throne from Lulach and reigned with his Queen for twenty happy years.

Malcolm Canmore's Scottish Family Tree is very ancient. He is descended directly from the first King of the Scots and Picts, Kenneth the son of Alpin. The name

Angus Turbech of Tara
Fiachu Fer-Mara
Ailill Erand
Feradach
Forgo
Maour
Aruail
Ro-Thrir
Trir
Ro-Sin
Sin
Dedad   **Scottish Royal line (Alpin)**
Iar   **from CHRONICLE OF KINGS**
Ailill
Eogan
Eterscel
Conaire-Mor
Admor   **Ancient King-list**
Coirpre   **recited in the**
Daire Dorn-Mor   **halls of the**
Coipre Crom-Chend   **Kings**
Ellatig
Lugaid
Mug-Lama
Conaire
Eochaid Riata

Fiachra Cathmail
Eochaid Antoit
Achroir
Findfece
Cruitlinde
Sen-Chormac
Fedlimid Ruamuach
Angus Buidnech
Fedlimid Aislingech
Angus Fir
Eochaid Muin-Remor

ERC

MacAlpin is still widely known today. Kenneth is descended from a king known as Erc and if we trace thirty-seven names beyond Erc we find Angus Turbech of Tara, showing that these people came originally from Ireland.

References:
Dictionary of National Biography
Anglo-Saxon Chronicle translated by Dorothy Whitelock
Early Sources of Scottish History by Alan Orr Anderson (2 volumes)

9

ALFRED THE GREAT AND THE ANGLO-SAXON CHRONICLES

QUEEN Margaret of Scotland was an Anglo-Saxon princess directly descended from Alfred the Great (848—900). This man was a very great King; though he only ruled over Wessex during his lifetime, he paved the way for future unification by his wise policies. England at that time was divided into seven kingdoms often at war with each other: Northumbria, Mercia, Essex, Sussex, East Anglia, Kent and Wessex. When he was quite a young boy his mother was reading aloud a volume of Saxon poetry to her four sons. She promised the book to the child who could read it first. Alfred who had not yet been taught his letters, rushed to his tutor and begged to have lessons. Though he was the youngest it was he who could recite it first and thus claim his reward. He was also loved by the people 'above his brothers, because in look, speech and in manners he was more graceful than they'.

When he became king, Alfred was obliged to fight many battles against fierce marauding Danes who constantly invaded southern England. When at long last he defeated them he showed his true greatness. He forgave their treachery, fed their starving soldiers, and offered them Christian baptism and a portion of the very country they had so cruelly ravaged. He was too wise to try and expel them completely since many Danes had been settled in the north for a long time. England, he felt, was big enough for the two races, if only they could live in peace.

Yet it was in peace rather than in war that Alfred's triumph lay. He restored ruined monasteries, he established a school for teaching the sons of freemen and thegns (nobles) to read; he even forced their astonished fathers to take lessons. He himself translated Christian literature into Anglo-Saxon, including the first fifty psalms. It was he who inspired the writing of the very important Anglo-Saxon chronicle which has been used so often in the preparation of this book. He encouraged craftsmen to come from many countries to work in precious metals.

When we travel backwards in time from Alfred we find that his great-grandfather Ealhmund was King of Kent in 784. Each of the seven kingdoms was ruled over by a king of the royal Anglo-Saxon line. These men were closely related by blood. In 560 A.D. Kent was ruled by Ethelbert. We do not know, owing to the anarchy of the times, his exact relationship to Alfred, but both were descended from Hengist and Horsa, the Saxons who invaded Britain in the fifth century, and both were descended from Woden, a chieftain who had taken the name of a god, the father of the gods in Norse mythology.

Ethelbert of Kent, great grandson of Hengist, had a

'glorious reign of fifty-six years', holding sway over all the provinces south of the Humber. He introduced a code of laws inspired by the Romans and was considered a great and wise king. His people the Jutes, originally from Jutland, were no barbarians. We still have the work of their jewellers and goldsmiths in our museums. They had reached a high level of culture for their time.

Ethelbert was not a Christian when the Roman missionary Augustine landed in Thanet in 579 A.D. He received the visitors courteously but in the open air in case a spell should be cast upon him. He did not at once agree to baptism but put no obstacles in the way of the monks. They could live in Canterbury and preach freely, though no one must be forced into an unwilling conversion. 'Your words and promises are fair indeed, but they are new and uncertain,' said the prudent king. Eventually however, inspired by the wonderful example of his guests, who lived holy and unworldly lives, Ethelbert was baptized. Bede, the Anglo-Saxon historian writing in Latin, declared that he was the 'first English king to enter the kingdom of Heaven'.

Anglo-Saxon Chronicles

These early chronicles are very important sources of information. They were histories written down, usually by monks because they could read and write, at the very time the actual events were happening. Sometimes they were written in Latin like the history of the Venerable Bede, but since Alfred's time much writing was done in the native Anglo-Saxon tongue, the forerunner of modern English. They were not dry-as-dust catalogues but very human documents as these extracts will show:

A.D.

671 In this year there was the great mortality of birds.

685 In this year there occurred in Britain bloody rain; milk and butter were turned to blood.

700 There was great frost this year so that the lakes and rivers of Ireland froze; the sea froze between Ireland and Scotland, so that there was communication between them on sheet ice.

793 In this year dire portents appeared over Northumbria and sorely frightened the people. They consisted of immense whirlwinds and flashes of lightning and fiery dragons were seen flying in the air.

1005 In this year occurred the great famine throughout England such as no man remembered one so cruel.

1100 Blood came bubbling out of the earth in Berkshire.

1106 Two moons appeared in the sky before Easter.

Noah
Sceaf   **Anglo-Saxon Royal Line**
Bedwig   **from Anglo-Saxon Chronicles**
Hwala
Hathra
Itermon
Heremod
Sceldwea
Beaw
Teatwa
Geat
Godwulf   **Anglo-Saxon King-list**
Finn   **recited in the halls**
Frithuwulf   **of the Kings**
Erealaf
Frithuwald
WODEN c 300
Baldwaeg
Brond or Brand
Frithogar

Freawine
Wig
Giwis
Esla
Elesa

CERDIC c 500
  first Saxon king of Britain
Cynric r 534
Cealwin r 560
Cuthwine
Cuthwulf
Ceowald
Cenred

It seems that our ancestors led quite exciting lives. We may well wonder what some of these 'dire portents' really were.

The Anglo-Saxon chronicles also contained pedigrees of kings taking them back to the beginning of time. Alfred was descended from Cerdic, the first Saxon king in Britain (500 A.D.), Hengist and Horsa came in the middle of the fifth century, and four generations still further back in time is Woden, the chieftain who had taken the name of a god. Fifteen generations before Woden we find Sceaf, who appears at the head of all the Anglo-Saxon pedigrees. Sceaf was the legendary founder of the race ... 'the mystic child washed up on the shores alone'. The present Queen Elizabeth of Britain is descended from these chieftains. The next name on her pedigree at Hatfield House before Sceaf is Noah and beyond Noah comes Adam, the first man. The chronicle states in all seriousness that Sceaf was born on the Ark. Legend has taken over from history at this point. Noah could never have travelled to these northern shores, even in so seaworthy a vessel as the Ark, which he had built himself.

At funeral ceremonies, or when chieftains were chosen, these impressive name-rolls were recited in the great wooden halls. Before people could read or write these pedigrees were memorized and handed down by word of mouth. Sagas and ballads too were sung or declaimed while bards and minstrels played their harps. Women served in drinking horns a sweet beverage known as mead, which was made of honey. Around the blazing log fire the warriors feasted, listened to the exciting stories of their ancestors, and dreamed of heroic deeds to come.

References:
Makers of the Realm by Arthur Bryant published by Collins
The Anglo-Saxon Chronicle translated by Dorothy Whitelock

10

ROBERT THE DEVIL AND EMMA
OF NORMANDY

USING our master key we can now open doors in the
family corridor of Normandy, where we first meet William the Conqueror, direct ancestor of Edward I. (See
Chart 8A.) William's earliest forbear was Ivar, the Jarl
or Earl of the Uplanders of Norway. These men were
originally Vikings. The word Viking comes from the
Norse *Vikingr*, which means pirate or buccaneer. These
wild seafaring raiders in their long ships with dragon-
shaped prows were the terror of civilized Europe. Prayers
were uttered in churches: 'From the fury of the North-
men Good Lord deliver us.'

Ivar's great-grandson was Rollo (846–932 A.D.) a
colourful character. Charles the Simple of France, real-
izing that he could not drive this Norse chieftain from
his realm, decided to turn Normandy over to him. The
Archbishop of Rouen came with advisers to state the

king's terms. Rollo must do homage for Normandy and swear an oath of loyalty to Charles, his liege lord. Rollo was quite willing until he was told that he would have to kiss the king's foot. This he refused to do: 'I will never bend my knee to anyone or kiss any man's foot.' Finally he yielded to the entreaties of the Archbishop and ordered one of his warriors to do the necessary kissing. The soldier seized Charles' foot and tipping him up gave the required kiss while the king lay flat on his back. Poor Charles, whose nickname merely meant that he was naïve, not mentally handicapped, had to be content with this rough and ready homage.

Though Rollo settled in fertile Normandy and was baptized a Christian, he retained the pagan custom of possessing more than one wife. However to consolidate his new position he legally married Gisela, daughter of Charles the Simple. Their son, William Longsword, became in due course Duke of Normandy in succession to his father. William could speak the old Norwegian language because Rollo had sent him to a special school at Bayeux to learn the speech of his ancestors. This was the same Bayeux where the famous tapestry depicting the Norman Conquest is to be found. Evidently these wild men from the north did not want to lose touch with their past. William Longsword's son was Richard the Fearless and *he* had a son Richard II of Normandy. Richard's II's son was an extraordinary person known sometimes as Robert the Magnificent and sometimes as Robert the Devil. This Robert was the father of William the Conqueror.

Robert the Devil

Robert the Devil was a man of almost superhuman strength. He was tall, golden-haired and had a powerful voice. Legend said that he had been born in answer to prayers which his mother had addressed to the Devil, hence his nickname. He took possession of Normandy by poisoning the rightful heir, his brother Richard III. Robert's fierceness and his prowess in battle (mostly against rebellious vassals) gave rise to so many legends that it is difficult to sift fact from fiction.

The story is told that, repenting of his crimes, Robert sought the advice of the Pope who directed him to a hermit. This holy man imposed on him a severe penance: he must pretend to be mad, he must only eat food dropped from the mouth of a dog, he must allow the common people to insult and ill-treat him without fighting back. How hard this must have been for such a strong hot-tempered man. He finally went to the Holy Land on a pilgrimage, and died on the way home from Jerusalem in 1035. He had been deeply in love with Arletta, the daughter of a tanner. Their son was the William duke of Normandy who conquered England in 1066.

Chart 10A

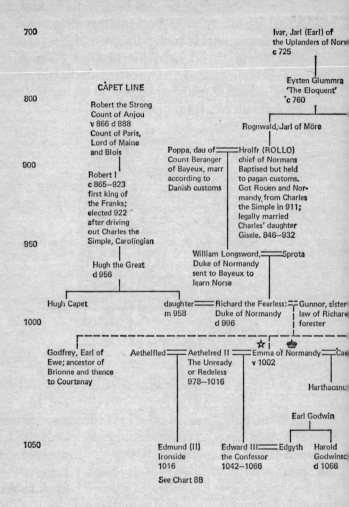

700 — Ivar, Jarl (Earl) of the Uplanders of Norw⋯ c 725

Eysten Glummra 'The Eloquent' c 760

CAPET LINE

800

Robert the Strong
Count of Anjou
v 866 d 888
Count of Paris,
Lord of Maine
and Blois

Rognwald, Jarl of Möre

Poppa, dau of===Hrolfr (ROLLO)
Count Beranger | chief of Normans
of Bayeux, marr | Baptised but held
according to | to pagan customs.
Danish customs | Got Rouen and Nor-
mandy from Charles
the Simple in 911;
legally married
Charles' daughter
Gisele. 846–932

900

Robert I
c 865–923
first king of
the Franks;
elected 922
after driving
out Charles the
Simple, Carolingian

950

William Longsword,===Sprota
Duke of Normandy
sent to Bayeux to
learn Norse

Hugh the Great
d 956

Hugh Capet   daughter===Richard the Fearless:==Gunnor, sister
              m 958   Duke of Normandy | law of Richar⋯
1000   d 996 | forester

Godfrey, Earl of   Aethelfled===Aethelred II   ☆ | ♛
Ewe; ancestor of   The Unready   ==Emma of Normandy===Ca⋯
Brionne and thence   or Redeless   v 1002
to Courtenay   978–1016
                                                      Harthacanu⋯

Earl Godwin

1050

Edmund (II)   Edward III===Edgyth   Harold
Ironside   the Confessor   Godwinso⋯
1016   1042–1066   d 1066

See Chart 8B

1100

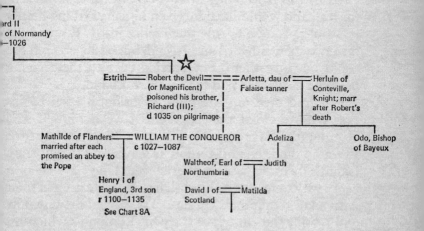

rick
stor of great
i line

ard II
of Normandy
–1026

☆

Estrith══Robert the Devil══ ══Arletta, dau of ══Herluin of
         (or Magnificent)   Falaise tanner   Conteville,
         poisoned his brother,   Knight; marr
         Richard (III);   after Robert's
         d 1035 on pilgrimage   death

Mathilde of Flanders══WILLIAM THE CONQUEROR   Adeliza   Odo, Bishop
married after each   c 1027–1087   of Bayeux
promised an abbey to
the Pope   Waltheof, Earl of ══Judith
                                  Northumbria
   Henry I of
   England, 3rd son   David I of ══Matilda
   r 1100–1135   Scotland

   See Chart 8A

Emma of Normandy

Richard the Fearless, grandfather of Robert the Devil, had also a daughter called Emma. If you study the chart you will see that she is the great-aunt of William the Conqueror. The chronicler, Henry Hastings, who tells her story, remarks that she was 'beautiful, accomplished, the gem of the Norman race'. She certainly had an eventful history. She is not as lovable as her step-great-granddaughter Margaret of Scotland, but life was hard for her.

In the spring of 1002 A.D. Emma came over the sea from Normandy to marry the English king, Ethelred the Unready. This man was soft, weak, vacillating and often unfaithful to his wife. The chronicler speaks bitterly of the bad policies of this king. 'The Danes were never offered tribute in time nor fought against; but when they had done most to our injury peace and truce were made with them.' The money paid to buy them off, called the Danegeld, crippled the country. However when Ethelred fled to Normandy after a defeat, the English sent for him and would have forgiven him everything if only he would promise to rule them more justly. Emma bore him two sons, Edward and Alfred, but oddly enough she could not love them. She carried over to these young boys the dislike she had felt for her husband.

Ethelred died and Edmund Ironside, his son by his first wife, divided the kingdom between himself and Canute, the invading Danish king. Soon afterwards Edmund died too and Canute was ruler of all England. Canute then did some rather clever things. He tried in every way to make the English like him. He upheld their native laws, punished wrong-doers, coined new money, and rebuilt the church of Bury St. Edmund's which his own people the Danes had destroyed in one of their fierce raids many years before, when they had killed

King Edmund of East Anglia because he would not re-
nounce Christianity (A.D. 869)

The story of Canute and the waves is well-known.
Some flattering courtiers had told him that even the sea
would obey such a wise king. So Canute sat at the mouth
of the Thames and let the high tide wash over his feet to
show that he was mortal like other men.

One day a bright idea came to this wily man. 'Sup-
pose I were to have as Queen a woman whom the English already know and love? What about that beautiful
Emma, widow of Ethelred, who is now in Normandy?
If the ordinary folk saw her again they would think that
a real English king sat on their throne. If *she* were to give
me a son, then surely they would accept him when I am
gone.'

So it was arranged. Emma came over to England and
married Canute. Then a strange thing happened.
Emma who had been so unhappy with Ethelred the Unready and was now brought over the sea once more like a
chattel, a pawn in a game of politics, found herself falling in love with this strong masterful Danish king.
Perhaps his physical appearance helped. 'He was huge
of limb, of great strength, a very goodly man to look
upon, save for his nose which was narrow, lofty and
hooked. He had long fair hair and bright keen eyes.'
When his coffin was opened years later he was found to
be a majestic imposing figure, still wearing a crown.

Canute for his part must have loved his wife dearly.
He loaded her with silver and gold and jewellery; he also
gave her rich estates near Winchester for her own
private possession. Emma did indeed bear him a son,
Hardacanute, whom she loved far better than her other
sons, but nothing went smoothly. When Canute died a
man called Harold Harefoot (he must have been as swift
as an Olympic runner) claimed that he was the King's

son by his first wife, Aelgifu. Harold did not like Emma who had replaced his mother so he seized her 'best treasures'. Then in 1037, when he was chosen king because Hardacanute stayed too long in Denmark, Harold Harefoot drove Emma out 'without mercy to face the raging winter'. The lady went over the sea to relatives in Belgium.

In 1040 Harold died so the English begged Hardacanute to come from Denmark to rule them. It turned out to be an unwise move for Hardacanute taxed them severely and ravaged the country when they resisted the tax-collectors. He also dug up the body of Harold Harefoot and threw it into a fen. However this new king did not live long to enjoy his power. He died of convulsions after heavy drinking in 1042.

Now who should succeed to the throne? The English chose Prince Edward, elder son of Emma and Ethelred, who had been driven to take refuge in Normandy while

Canute was reigning. He became Edward
ruling England for twenty-three years. 1
speaks of him in glowing terms:

'Noble in goodness, pure and upright,
Edward the glorious, guarding his homelar

His mother still could not like him. She was now back
in England and in possession of her former estates. She
began to plot with Magnus King of Norway, giving him
treasure and inviting him to invade England and seize
the throne. Edward the Confessor was not a cruel man,
but he could not tolerate such behaviour. He allowed his
mother to remain quietly at Winchester, but he took
away her land, her gold and silver and 'Things beyond
description.' The chronicler does not mince his words:
'While he (Edward the Confessor) was reigning in peace
like unto Solomon, his own mother plotted with
Magnus, King of Norway. Wherefore this traitor to the
kingdom, this enemy of the country, this betrayer of her
own son, was judged and everything she possessed was
forfeited to the king.'

In 1051 Emma died. She was buried in the old Minster
beside Canute at Winchester. This ancient building
collapsed in 1107. Her bones were then transferred to a
mortuary chest in the present cathedral and in the nineteenth century a sculptor made a statue of her. So the
beautiful Emma of Normandy has not been entirely forgotten.

References:
Anglo-Saxon Chronicle translated by Dorothy Whitelock
Dictionary of National Biography
Encyclopedia Britannica

11

THE CAROLINGIAN LINE

THE Normans were linked through marriage to powerful and important people known as the Carolingians. They acquire this name from their most famous representative, Charlemagne or Charles the Great. The Carolingians were not of the 'blood royal' but had been the power behind the throne when the kings of Frankland or France, the Merovingians, had become weak and degenerate. These Mayors of the Palace, as this dynamic family came to be called, included a famous warrior Charles Martel or the Hammer, who defeated the Turks at the Battle of Tours in 732 A.D., and Martel's son Pippin the Short, a skilful statesman who was finally crowned King of the Franks in 754. This Pippin was the father of Charles the Great, or Charlemagne.

Charlemagne

Charlemagne (742–814 A.D.) is one of the great figures of history. Throughout his long reign he was constantly fighting. Sometimes he had to fight in self-defence against wild tribes like the Saxons who were always attacking his territory. He tried to force Christianity on these people and when they refused to be baptized he beheaded four thousand in one day. This seems terribly cruel to us but in those days it was thought right to destroy the opponents of the Christian religion. The Avars of Hungary often attacked the kingdom and by sea and land there was a long warfare with the Saracens until peace was signed with the Emir of Cordova in 810.

In these wars Roland and Oliver, two devoted friends, always fought side by side. Roland was Charlemagne's

nephew who went with him into Spain to help fight the
Saracens. On the way back Roland and his followers
were trapped in the Pass of Roncesvalles, as they were

crossing the Pyrenees. Roland had agreed to sound his
magic horn of carved ivory should he need help from his
uncle who had ridden on ahead. For hours the heroes
defended the Pass against attack, Roland performing
great deeds of valour with his famous sword Durendal.
Though hard-pressed by the enemy Roland was too
proud to call for help. As he lay wounded on the battle-
field the young warrior remembered with nostalgia the
fair land of France. In poignant words he offered his
right glove to God, his supreme liege lord.

When at last the notes of the magic horn came faintly
over the wind Charlemagne turned back, but it was too
late. Roland and Oliver lay dead amid their brave com-
panions, but before he died Roland had heard Charlemagne's great battle-cry 'Montjoie' (My Joy) and
knew that help was on the way. All these exciting events

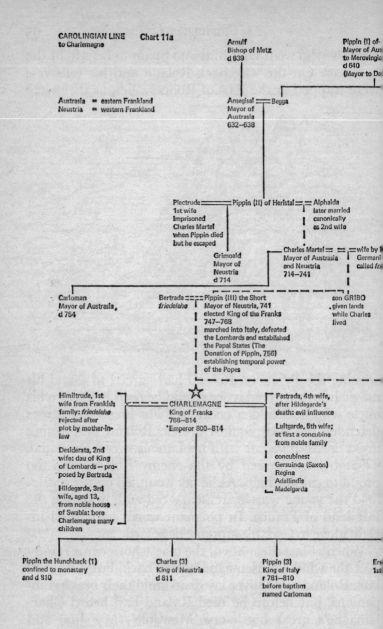

CAROLINGIAN LINE
to Charlemagne   Chart 11a

Arnulf
Bishop of Metz
d 639

Pippin (I) of-
Mayor of Aus
to Merovingia
d 640
(Mayor to Da

Austrasia = eastern Frankland
Neustria = western Frankland

Ansegisal ══ Begga
Mayor of
Austrasia
632–638

Plectrude ═══════ Pippin (II) of Heristal ══ ═ Alphaida
1st wife   later married
imprisoned   canonically
Charles Martel   as 2nd wife
when Pippin died
but he escaped

Grimoald
Mayor of
Neustria
d 714

Charles Martel ══ ═ ══wife by
Mayor of Austrasia   Germani
and Neustria   called *fr*
714–741

Carloman
Mayor of Austrasia,
d 754

Bertrada ════ Pippin (III) the Short
friedelehe   Mayor of Neustria, 741
              elected King of the Franks
              747–768
              marched into Italy, defeated
              the Lombards and established
              the Papal States (The
              Donation of Pippin, 756)
              establishing temporal power
              of the Popes

son GRIBO
given lands
while Charles
lived

Himiltrude, 1st
wife from Frankish
family: *friedelehe*
rejected after
plot by mother-in-
law

Desiderata, 2nd
wife: dau of King
of Lombards — pro-
posed by Bertrada

Hildegarde, 3rd
wife, aged 13,
from noble house
of Swabia: bore
Charlemagne many
children

☆ ══ CHARLEMAGNE ══
King of Franks
768–814
*Emperor 800–814

Fastrada, 4th wife,
after Hildegarde's
death: evil influence

Luitgarde, 5th wife;
at first a concubine
from noble family

concubines:
Gersuinda (Saxon)
Regina
Adallindis
Madelgarda

Pippin the Hunchback (1)
confined to monastery
and d 810

Charles (3)
King of Neustria
d 811

Pippin (3)
King of Italy
r 781–810
before baptism
named Carloman

Er
1st

ald
of Austrasia
usurp the
ngian crown
killed by
nks in 656,
ting anew
ngian power

bert
f Austrasia

an
Austrasia
771

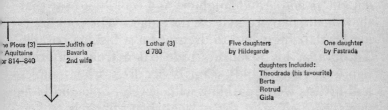

e Pious (3) === Judith of	Lothar (3)	Five daughters	One daughter
Aquitaine Bavaria	d 780	by Hildegarde	by Fastrada
or 814—840 2nd wife			

daughters included:
Theodrada (his favourite)
Berta
Rotrud
Gisla

are related in the *Song of Roland*, an epic poem written in old French. Taillefer, a French minstrel, chanted this very poem at the Battle of Hastings, to encourage the invading Normans.

Charlemagne's peaceful achievements were equally important. He admired scholars so he invited a learnéd monk from England called Alcuin to reside at his court. At this epoch English monks were considered the best educated men in Europe. Abbey schools were founded to teach the nobles to read. Though he could read, Charlemagne himself never mastered the art of writing.

At Aix la Chapelle Charlemagne built a wonderful palace decorated with mosaics and marbles brought from Italy. This lively and energetic man took an interest in everything: astronomy, farming, even bee-keeping. A story is told that, when he was seven, he saw the coffin of a saint move of its own accord into its tomb and give off a sweet perfume. This episode made a deep impression on him. He remembered the day because it was then that he had lost one of his baby teeth. When I was young children used to be paid a 6d (2½p) for each milktooth safely extracted. Charlemagne's strong interest in religion dated from this time. He would visit his church several times a day and even during the night.

Charlemagne was at his most natural with his family. He had married several wives at different times and had a large number of children. Especially did he love his daughters and granddaughters and could not bear that they should marry and leave the palace. When out hunting his daughters had to dress as for a fashion parade. Theodrada, his favourite, rode out a truly glittering figure: 'her feet, hands, seams of her dresses, her temples and breasts were sparkling with jewels'. Splendid banquets were given in the palace when minstrels recited epic poems describing heroic deeds. Always the girls were present at their father's side. Though the feasts were lavish, drunkenness was never allowed.

We know what this extraordinary king looked like because his faithful friend Einhard left us a vivid description. Charlemagne was six feet three and a half inches tall with large vivacious eyes and a jolly happy-looking face. He had a high-pitched voice for such a big man and he tended to splutter as he spoke; the words and ideas simply pouring out. He liked friends to come and chat even when he was in the bath. He was a magnificent swimmer. We should certainly now call him an extrovert. His coffin was opened in 1861, when his skeleton revealed a splendid physique.

On Christmas Day 800 A.D. the Pope placed another crown on Charlemagne's head. This time he was

Chart 11b

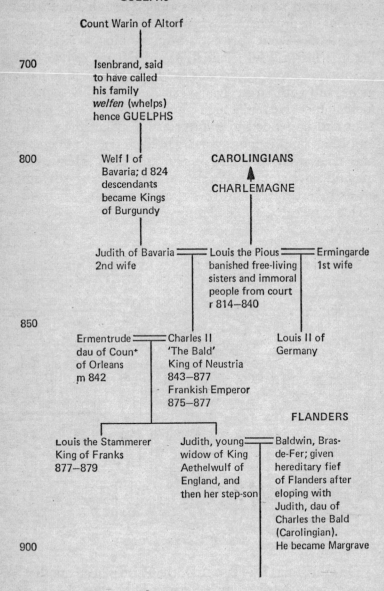

GUELPHS

Count Warin of Altorf

700

Isenbrand, said
to have called
his family
welfen (whelps)
hence GUELPHS

800

Welf I of
Bavaria; d 824
descendants
became Kings
of Burgundy

CAROLINGIANS

CHARLEMAGNE

Judith of Bavaria ══ Louis the Pious ══ Ermingarde
2nd wife   banished free-living   1st wife
                   sisters and immoral
                   people from court
                   r 814—840

850

Ermentrude ══ Charles II   Louis II of
dau of Coun⁺   'The Bald'   Germany
of Orleans   King of Neustria
m 842   843—877
               Frankish Emperor
               875—877

FLANDERS

Louis the Stammerer   Judith, young ══ Baldwin, Bras-
King of Franks   widow of King   de-Fer; given
877—879   Aethelwulf of   hereditary fief
                   England, and   of Flanders after
                   then her step-son   eloping with
                                    Judith, dau of
                                    Charles the Bald
                                    (Carolingian).
                                    He became Margrave

900

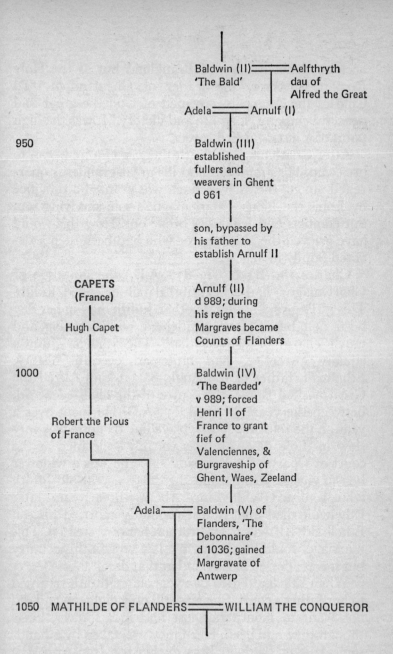

Baldwin (II)══════Aelfthryth
'The Bald'　　　　dau of
　　　　　　　　Alfred the Great

Adela══════Arnulf (I)

950　　Baldwin (III)
　　　established
　　　fullers and
　　　weavers in Ghent
　　　d 961

　　　son, bypassed by
　　　his father to
　　　establish Arnulf II

CAPETS　　　Arnulf (II)
(France)　　d 989; during
　　　　　　his reign the
Hugh Capet　Margraves became
　　　　　　Counts of Flanders

1000　　Baldwin (IV)
　　　'The Bearded'
　　　v 989; forced
　　　Henri II of
Robert the Pious　France to grant
of France　　fief of
　　　　　　Valenciennes, &
　　　　　　Burgraveship of
　　　　　　Ghent, Waes, Zeeland

Adela══════Baldwin (V) of
　　　　　　Flanders, 'The
　　　　　　Debonnaire'
　　　　　　d 1036; gained
　　　　　　Margravate of
　　　　　　Antwerp

1050　MATHILDE OF FLANDERS══════WILLIAM THE CONQUEROR

acclaimed not as king of Frankland but as the Holy Roman Emperor, the leader of Christendom. 'To Charles the Augustus, crowned of God the great and peaceful emperor, long life and victory.' It was the high point of a distinguished career.

After Charlemagne's death the vast empire began to break up. His grandsons and his great-grandsons quarrelled among themselves. Each was granted a province by Louis the Pious, Charlemagne's sole surviving son, but conflicts and jealousies broke out. How this would have grieved the old emperor who had been such a devoted family man.

Charles the Bald (823–877 A.D.) the grandson of Charlemagne, had a beautiful daughter called Judith. This girl's grandmother, another Judith, had in her day been noted for 'piety, gentleness, wide learning and much charm of conversation'. The younger Judith, equally attractive, had quite an eventful history. Ethelwulf, father of the Anglo-Saxon king Alfred the Great, visited Rome, the centre of the civilized world, between the years 853 and 855 A.D. He spent over a year on the return journey; travelling by horse was very slow in those days. He was warmly welcomed at the court of Charles the Bald and since he was a widower he was given a young bride, the thirteen-year-old Judith who returned with him. About three years later Ethelwulf died and Judith promptly married his son Ethelbald, Alfred's older brother, her own stepson. This marriage would be against the law now in this country but it was allowed in England at that date.

When Ethelbald died two years later Judith returned to her father's court. She was still only eighteen and did not want to mourn her lost husbands forever, kings though they had been. Her fancy was taken by a handsome knight, Baldwin Bras de Fer, or Iron-Arm. His nickname shows how brave and strong he must have been. Baldwin had no land or money to speak of, only his strong right arm – of iron – to recommend him. The young couple fell deeply in love and decided to elope. Charles the Bald was furious at this poor match, but at last he agreed to make the best of it. He gave Baldwin the rich province of Flanders as a wedding present. Their son Baldwin the Bald (he seems to have taken after grandpa) married Aelfthryth, the daughter of Alfred the Great, so Judith had not forgotten her English relations.

There follows a line of Baldwins and Arnulfs. Baldwin III, great-grandson of Judith, established textile workers and weavers at Ghent, thus increasing the prosperity of his small industrious country. Baldwin V, great-great-great-great-great-grandson of Judith, called le Debonnair, which means that he was gay, courteous and civilized, became very powerful. He added Antwerp to his possessions and was regent in France to Philip I. This Baldwin lived to see his daughter Matilda sharing the English throne with William the Conqueror, Duke of Normandy. Thus descent can be traced from Charlemagne and from Ivar the Norseman, ancestor of the first Norman king of England.

References:
Encyclopedia of World History edited by William L. Langer
Carolingian Empire by H. Fichtenau
Encyclopedia Britannica
Dictionary of National Biography

12

THE MEROVINGIAN LINE: A MONSTER AT THE TOP OF THE TREE

THERE is one last family with which a link can be formed, far back in the Dark Ages, and that is the Merovingian line. Bertha, the Christian wife of Ethelbert of Kent, was a Merovingian princess, daughter of the King of Paris. This connection can be established in two ways: either through King Ethelbert of Kent, or through Queen Eleanor, wife of Henry II who was descended from the house of Aquitaine and goes directly back in her own right to the Merovingians. The name Merovech means 'sea-born' and with Prince Merovech the Merovingian line begins. His mother was a princess but legend has it that his father was a monster with horns on his head who came out of the sea and took the princess who was resting on the sea-shore. So there could really be a monster at the top of this Family Tree. Certainly many of the Merovingians (descendants of Merovech) showed a monster-like cruelty.

Childerich I, the son of Merovech, behaved so badly

that his subjects expelled him from the kingdom. He took
refuge with King Bisinus and Queen Basina in Thuringia
(part of what is now Germany). Later Childeric was
allowed to return to his own realm. To his surprise Queen
Basina soon came to join him and they were married. 'I
know thee capable and strenuous in action, therefore
I am come to dwell with thee.' Had she found anyone
better beyond the sea she would have left her husband
to live with him, she declared with blunt simplicity.

A story is told by the Chronicler Fredegar which
reveals the restless nocturnal habits of this queen. Three
times she roused Childeric in the night, bidding him go
outside, note what he saw and bring her word again.
(My own husband would have taken a dim view of this
disturbance). The first time the king saw lions and
leopards (impossible even in ancient France); the second
time bears and wolves (more likely) and the third time
he saw some lesser beasts. 'Even so' declared his wife
'shall thy descendants be.' This prophecy was meant to
foretell the degenerate do-nothing kings who were to
follow in about three hundred years' time. It is exciting
to remember that Childeric's jewelled sword and gold
ornaments are now in the Cabinet des Médailles, a

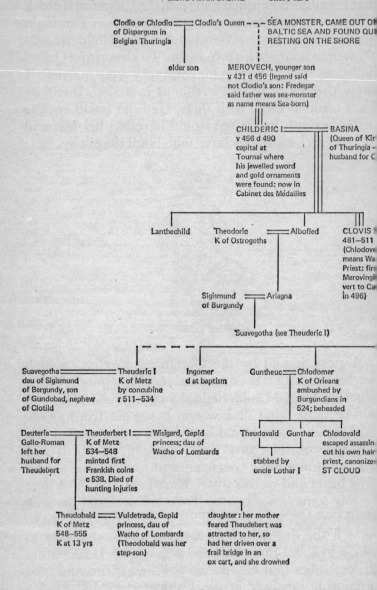

Clodio or Chlodio ══ Clodio's Queen ──┐── SEA MONSTER, CAME OUT O**N**
of Dispargum in   BALTIC SEA AND FOUND QU**I**
Belgian Thuringia   RESTING ON THE SHORE

           elder son   MEROVECH, younger son
                        v 431 d 456 (legend said
                        not Clodio's son: Fredegar
                        said father was sea-monster
                        as name means Sea-born)

CHILDERIC I ═══════ BASINA
v 456 d 490   (Queen of Kir
capital at   of Thuringia –
Tournai where   husband for C
his jewelled sword
and gold ornaments
were found: now in
Cabinet des Médailles

Lanthechild   Theodoric ══ Albofled   CLOVIS
                K of Ostrogoths   481–511
                                          (Chlodove
                                          means Wa
                                          Priest: firs
                                          Merovingi
                                          vert to Ca
                                          in 496)

                  Sigismund ══ Ariagna
                  of Burgundy

                  ˙Suavegotha (see Theuderic I)

Suavegotha ═══════ Theuderic I   Ingomer   Guntheuc ══ Chlodomer
dau of Sigismund   K of Metz   d at baptism   K of Orleans
of Bergundy, son   by concubine   ambushed by
of Gundobad, nephew   r 511–534   Burgundians in
of Clotild   524; beheaded

Deuteria ══════ Theuderbert I ══ Wisigard, Gepid   Theudovald   Gunthar   Chlodovald
Gallo-Roman   K of Metz   princess; dau of   escaped assassin
left her   534–548   Wacho of Lombards   cut his own hair
husband for   minted first   priest, canonize
Theudebert   Frankish coins   ST CLOUD
                 c 538. Died of   stabbed by
                 hunting injuries   uncle Lothar I

Theudobald ═══ Vuldetrada, Gepid   daughter : her mother
K of Metz   princess, dau of   feared Theudebert was
548–555   Wacho of Lombards   attracted to her, so
K at 13 yrs   (Theodobald was her   had her driven over a
                   step-son)   frail bridge in an
                                             ox cart, and she drowned

═ CLOTILD
  Dau of King
  Chilperic of
  Burgundy; he was
  murdered by his
  brother Gundobad:
  Clotild later had
  blood-feud vengeance
  on his descendants,
  Clotild & Clovis
  built Ste Geneviève
  where both are buried

...gotha ═══ Childebert I	LOTHAR I	Clotild ═══ Amalaric

...gotha ═══ Childebert I
  queen   K of Paris
 ...othar's   "best of sons
 ...he was re- of Clovis";
 ...y nephew   no male issue
 ...rt to live d of disease 545
  garden
 ... by Childebert
 ... daughters:
 ...rg & Chlothsind

LOTHAR I
  K of Soisson
  d 561

Lothar I with his brother
Childebert and nephew
Theudebert I extended
Merovingian Gaul to its
furthest extent; became
King of all Franks 558–561

for Lothar and his line
see next chart

Clotild ═══ Amalaric
           Visiogothic king

museum in Paris, where French children can see them at any time.

In 481 A.D. Childeric was succeeded by his son Clovis. Many picturesque stories are told about this king, though he could show great cruelty when thwarted. Once, when he was fighting the Romans, his troops plundered many churches of their ornaments. A bishop begged for the return of a large ewer or vase, so Clovis commanded his men to spare the vase and give it intact to the bishop. A careless or defiant soldier smashed it however so that only tiny pieces could be saved. Clovis did not forget this disobedience. For a year

he said nothing but during a military inspection he blamed this very soldier for his slovenly appearance and threw his axe to the ground. While the man, no doubt ashamed of the rebuke, was stooping to pick up his weapon Clovis took his own axe and split the man's skull, crying as he did so: 'Thus didst thou treat the ewer at Soissons.' This story of the *Soissons Vase* became famous and Clovis was greatly feared.

Later when Clovis was fighting the Visigoths (tribes from the east who were overrunning Europe) a miraculous hind or deer was said to have appeared to show him a ford in the river where he could cross. Then a globe of fire is supposed to have shone in the sky over Poitiers to help direct his march. Clovis had many victories over the Goths and this time the Romans approved of him for he was fighting their enemies too. He captured the Gothic capital of Toulouse and went on in triumph to Tours to be received by the Emperor Anastasius and created a Proconsul and Patrician, honours highly prized in Rome. He dressed in purple and scattered gold pieces to the crowds who were acclaiming him. He became still more powerful when he had overrun the province of another Frankish king, his cousin Sigibert. After these victories the Franks clashed their shields together and raised Clovis upon a shield. He was their hero, their conqueror, the ruler now of a vast territory in France.

Every time he was victorious Clovis captured from the Goths much booty and treasure. He even married a Gothic princess called Clothild, a lady renowned for her beauty, grace and wisdom. She was a Christian but the shrewd Clovis made a bargain with God. He would accept his wife's religion and be baptized if he were granted victory in a certain battle. His wish was granted so he honoured his pledge.

Clovis died in 511 A.D. and lies with his Queen in the ancient church of St. Geneviève in Paris which they had built together.

References:
Bede's *Ecclesiastical History*
Arthur Bryant's *Makers of the Realm*
Encyclopedia of World History ed. Langer
History of the Franks by Gregory of Tours translated by Dalton 1922

13

MORE MEROVINGIANS: MOST OF THEM WICKED

IN Merovingian times the young royal princes were noted for their long, golden hair. This long hair was a sign of their high rank. Some touching incidents are recorded which show the importance of this hair-style. The great warrior Clovis had left behind four sons: Theodoric, Chlodomer, Childebert, and Lothair I, who divided their father's immense domain into four kingdoms with four capitals: Metz, Orleans, Paris and Soissons. Many were the struggles and conflicts which arose between these brothers and their descendants. When Chlodomer, king of Orleans, was killed in battle in 524 A.D., his unscrupulous brother Lothair I schemed how to get rid of his nephews and annex their inheritance. So he showed a pair of shears to Clothild, the loving grandmother of the boys, who was now a widow. In despair she cried out: 'Better dead than shorn.' She could not bear the thought of these innocent young princes wearing their hair short like serfs or monks.

Two of the lads, Theudovald and Gunthar, were shorn and stabbed, but Chodovald, the third boy, was rescued by servants. He cut his hair of his own accord, entered a monastery and was later canonized. His name survives today in St. Cloud, a suburb of Paris. By these cruel methods Lothair I expanded his empire; with the help of his other brothers he finally drove the Visigoths down into Spain.

In later years another pathetic story reveals the social significance of the long hair. Guntram, king of Burgundy, (561–592 A.D.) was a childless son of Lothair I, but had a very different character. He suspected that two of his own nephews lay in unmarked paupers' graves. Their murder had been contrived by a ruthless sister-in-law. This dishonour filled Guntram with sorrow so he organized much digging and searching. At last two graves were uncovered and there lay two lads wearing the long golden hair of royal princes. The bodies could now receive a burial befitting their exalted rank.

Even in those early times when women were given in marriage for political reasons, many stand out for their charm and personality. The grasping king, Lothair I, had captured Radegund, niece of the King of Thuringia (west Germany) as part of the spoils of war, when she was only ten years old. When she was more mature he married her, but the little princess did not like her bridegroom, so she left him and founded a convent at Poitiers. She was later canonized for her charity and saintliness. In those days women who wanted to become well-educated and independent often entered convents.

Lothair I had numerous wives, which was not unusual then, even among men who were supposed to be Christians. One of these wives was a serf called Ingund. She in her turn asked Lothair to find an important husband for her sister Aregund. Lothair reported that he had

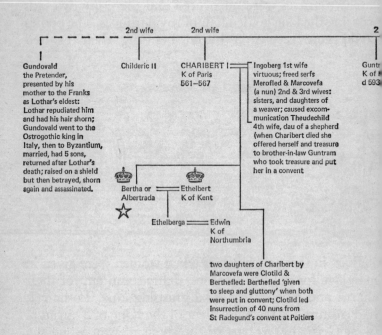

2nd wife   2nd wife   2

Gundovald
the Pretender,
presented by his
mother to the Franks
as Lothar's eldest:
Lothar repudiated him
and had his hair shorn;
Gundovald went to the
Ostrogothic king in
Italy, then to Byzantium,
married, had 5 sons,
returned after Lothar's
death; raised on a shield
but then betrayed, shorn
again and assassinated.

Childeric II

CHARIBERT I
K of Paris
561–567

Ingoberg 1st wife
virtuous; freed serfs
Merofled & Marcovefa
(a nun) 2nd & 3rd wives:
sisters, and daughters of
a weaver; caused excom-
munication Theudechild
4th wife, dau of a shepherd
(when Charibert died she
offered herself and treasure
to brother-in-law Guntram
who took treasure and put
her in a convent

Guntr
K of
d 593

Bertha or
Albertrada

Ethelbert
K of Kent

Ethelberga ═══ Edwin
K of
Northumbria

two daughters of Charibert by
Marcovefa were Clotild &
Berthefled: Berthefled 'given
to sleep and gluttony' when both
were put in convent; Clotild led
insurrection of 40 nuns from
St Radegund's convent at Poitiers

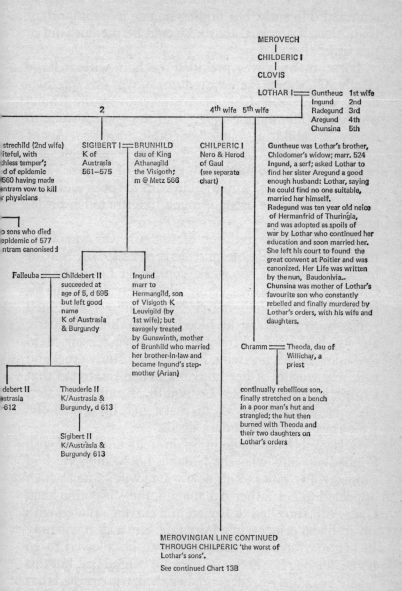

MEROVECH
|
CHILDERIC I
|
CLOVIS
|
LOTHAR I ═══ Guntheuc   1st wife
               Ingund   2nd
               Radegund 3rd
               Aregund   4th
               Chunsina 5th

2   4th wife   5th wife

...strechild (2nd wife)
...iteful, with
...thless temper';
...d of epidemic
...560 having made
...untram vow to kill
... physicians

SIGIBERT I ═══ BRUNHILD
K of   dau of King
Austrasia   Athanagild
561–575   the Visigoth;
          m @ Metz 566

CHILPERIC I
Nero & Herod
of Gaul
(see separate
chart)

Guntheuc was Lothar's brother,
Chlodomer's widow; marr. 524
Ingund, a serf; asked Lothar to
find her sister Aregund a good
enough husband: Lothar, saying
he could find no one suitable,
married her himself.
Radegund was ten year old neice
of Hermanfrid of Thuringia,
and was adopted as spoils of
war by Lothar who continued her
education and soon married her.
She left his court to found the
great convent at Poitier and was
canonized. Her Life was written
by the nun, Baudonivia.
Chunsina was mother of Lothar's
favourite son who constantly
rebelled and finally murdered by
Lothar's orders, with his wife and
daughters.

...o sons who died
...epidemic of 577
...ntram canonised ⅃

Faileuba ═══ Childebert II
            succeeded at
            age of 5, d 595
            but left good
            name
            K of Austrasia
            & Burgundy

Ingund
marr to
Hermangild, son
of Visigoth K
Leuvigild (by
1st wife); but
savagely treated
by Gunswinth, mother
of Brunhild who married
her brother-in-law and
became Ingund's step-
mother (Arian)

Chramm ═══ Theoda, dau of
            Willichar, a
            priest

...debert II
...ustrasia
...–612

Theuderic II
K/Austrasia &
Burgundy, d 613

continually rebellious son,
finally stretched on a bench
in a poor man's hut and
strangled; the hut then
burned with Theoda and
their two daughters on
Lothar's orders

Sigibert II
K/Austrasia &
Burgundy 613

MEROVINGIAN LINE CONTINUED
THROUGH CHILPERIC 'the worst of
Lothar's sons'.

See continued Chart 13B

searched diligently, but finding no one more important than himself, decided that he would be the husband of this sister also.

These many wives provided Lothair with a large family. Guntram, the devoted uncle, was one son. Sigibert, another son, King of Austrasia (near the Rhine) was also a fine man. Sigibert had the good fortune to marry Brunhild, a young Visigothic princess: 'A girl graceful of form, fair to look upon, honourable and comely, prudent in judgment, amiable of address.' This lady was also very learned; able both to speak and read Latin fluently. She brought much treasure to her bridegroom.

Chilperic I, the sixth son of Lothair, was one of the most evil men of all time, and has been called the Nero of his age, though he too was a competent Latin scholar. Chilperic was filled with envy when he realized that his brother Sigibert had married such an accomplished young woman of royal blood as Brunhild. Chilperic already had a wife, Fredegund, a former serving-maid to Audovera, his first wife. Fredegund, utterly cruel and evil, was worthy of her husband. When she found that Chilperic had sent for Galswinth, Brunhild's sister, another lovely princess, to make her his bride, the jealous woman plotted dark deeds.

Galswinth left Toledo in Spain 'reluctantly and with foreboding' and who shall blame her? Chilperic had promised five cities to his new young wife, a fact which appealed to her father Athanagild, the Visigothic king. Galswinth travelled to Rouen in a carriage plated with silver, like a princess in a fairy tale. She was so unhappy in her marriage that she begged to be allowed to go home, leaving her immense treasure behind her, but this would not satisfy Fredegund, her rival, who insisted that Chilperic should have her strangled.

Fredegund lost all her own sons except Lothair II by plague or fever. This sad fact filled her with temporary penitence and prompted her to burn her tenants' tax forms so that they would not have to pay the heavy sums demanded by Chilperic, but this new mood did not last long. It was on her orders that poor Brunhild, sister of the rival she so much hated, was paraded on a camel when she was quite an old lady, and then torn to pieces by wild horses. Those were savage times indeed.

King Chilperic and Queen Fredegund became the chief characters in an operetta, *Chilperic*, staged in Paris in 1868. The composer Hervé sang the part of the king. Fredegund was performed by one of the most colourful actresses of the time, Blanche d'Antigny, famous for her own personal treasure of diamonds. In her role as Fredegund, clad only in a sheepskin, she hurled in her husband's face his gifts of diamonds and jewelled belts. It seems that the French do not easily forget their dramatic ancient history.

It was this cruel pair however who continued the line, because Dagobert I, king of all the Franks from 629–639 A.D., their grandson, was the last strong Merovingian king. After that the Mayors of the Palace became the

Chart 13B

Visigothic connections with
Merovingians, and CHILPERIC
who extended the Merovingian
dynasty

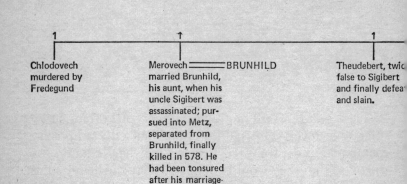

1	↑	1
Chlodovech murdered by Fredegund	Merovech ═══════ BRUNHILD married Brunhild, his aunt, when his uncle Sigibert was assassinated; pursued into Metz, separated from Brunhild, finally killed in 578. He had been tonsured after his marriage and sent to monastery of St Calais; escaped with faithful servant Gailen whom he begged to stab him when cornered. Gailen tortured and killed by Chilperic.	Theudebert, twic false to Sigibert and finally defea and slain.

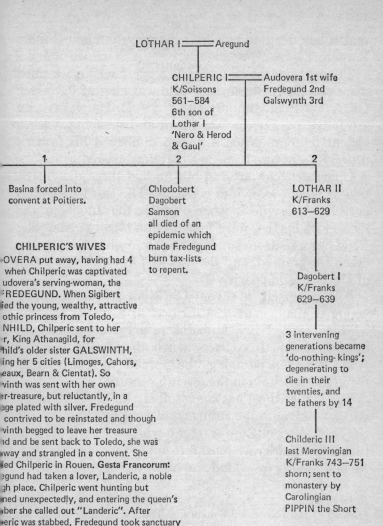

LOTHAR I══════Aregund

CHILPERIC I══════Audovera 1st wife
K/Soissons · · · · · · Fredegund 2nd
561—584 · · · · · · · Galswynth 3rd
6th son of
Lothar I
'Nero & Herod
& Gaul'

1 · · · · · · · · · **2** · · · · · · · · · **2**

Basina forced into · · · Chlodobert · · · · · LOTHAR II
convent at Poitiers. · · Dagobert · · · · · · K/Franks
· · · · · · · · · · · · · Samson · · · · · · · 613—629
· · · · · · · · · · · · · all died of an
· · · · · · · · · · · · · epidemic which
CHILPERIC'S WIVES · · made Fredegund
OVERA put away, having had 4 · burn tax-lists
when Chilperic was captivated · to repent.
udovera's serving-woman, the
FREDEGUND. When Sigibert · · · · · · · · · · · · Dagobert I
ied the young, wealthy, attractive · · · · · · · · K/Franks
othic princess from Toledo, · · · · · · · · · · · 629—639
NHILD, Chilperic sent to her
r, King Athanagild, for
hild's older sister GALSWINTH, · · · · · · · · · 3 intervening
ing her 5 cities (Limoges, Cahors, · · · · · · · generations became
eaux, Bearn & Cientat). So · · · · · · · · · · · 'do-nothing- kings';
vinth was sent with her own · · · · · · · · · · · degenerating to
er-treasure, but reluctantly, in a · · · · · · · · die in their
age plated with silver. Fredegund · · · · · · · · twenties, and
contrived to be reinstated and though · · · · · · be fathers by 14
vinth begged to leave her treasure
nd and be sent back to Toledo, she was
way and strangled in a convent. She · · · · · · Childeric III
ied Chilperic in Rouen. **Gesta Francorum:** · · last Merovingian
egund had taken a lover, Landeric, a noble · · · K/Franks 743—751
gh place. Chilperic went hunting but · · · · · · shorn; sent to
ned unexpectedly, and entering the queen's · · · monastery by
ber she called out "Landeric". After · · · · · · Carolingian
eric was stabbed, Fredegund took sanctuary · · · PIPPIN the Short
ris with all the royal treasure she could lay
s on, and begged Guntram to be guardian
r youngest infant, LOTHAR II, who
nued the Merovingian line.

real rulers, leading to Charlemagne, the Holy Roman Emperor.

There is one more son of Lothair I whom we must mention. He is Charibert I who was king of Paris (see Chart 13A) between 561 and 567 A.D. He was not an attractive person; he was mean and grasping, with a violent temper. When a bishop disobeyed his father's orders he sent him home in a cart lined with thorns.

Charibert had no sons, but he had three daughters, two of whom went into convents. The third daughter, born from his wife Ingoberg, was Bertha. Ingoberg, the mother of Bertha, must have been a sweet person. She freed her serfs from bondage at a time when slavery was taken for granted, and she was well-known for her acts of kindness and charity.

Bertha herself, a devout Christian and a charming young woman, married Ethelbert of Kent. It was she who persuaded her husband to receive the Roman missionaries with courtesy when they landed in 597 A.D., thus encouraging the spread of Christianity throughout Britain in the seventh century.

So ... the wheel has come full circle. We have made our last link with the strange and exciting characters of the Dark Ages of Europe. If the cruelty of some of them makes us shudder we must remember that, against fearful odds, many were kind and many were courageous.

References:
History of the Franks by Gregory of Tours translated by Dalton
    1922

Visigoth family of
Brunhild & Galswinth

Athanagild	Gunswinth or	Leuvigild	1st wife	Leuva
K/Spain (1)	Goiswinth or	(2) finally K		died young;
d 567–8	Godeswinth	of all Spain		his power
	(Arian)			taken by
				Leuvigild

BRUNHILD
queen of Sigibert
m @ Metz, 566
'girl of graceful form
honourable, and comely
to look upon, prudent
in judgment, amiable of
address': came with great
Spanish & Burgundian treasure to Metz, capital of
Austrasia; convert to
Catholicism

Galswinth
3rd wife of
Chilperic;
assassinated
at instigation
of Fredegund

Hermangild ═══ Ingund, dau of
killed by   Sigibert & Brunhild
his father   was savagely treated
for accept-   by her step-mother,
ing Catholicism Gunswinth (Arian);
on marrying   'people hired to
Ingund   hurl filth at her
                 on way to mass; and
                 finally dragged by the
                 hair and injured. She
                 sent her bloodied
                 handkerchief to her
                 uncle Guntram'. After
                 Hermangild's death she
                 and her son sent to Africa
                 where she died; her young
                 son reached Constantinople.

Recared (brother/Hermangild)
betrothed to
Rigunth, dau of
Chilperic &
Fredegund.
(Rigunth's mother
told her to see the
treasures in a huge
chest, and tried to
shut the lid upon
her neck.) On
Chilperic's murder
Rigunth's treasure was
seized before she
reached Spain, by Duke
Desiderius near Avignon
in 584.

Recared later sought
hand of another sister,
Chlosind, but Guntram
refused because of the
treatment of Ingund.

14

THE MYSTERY OF THE MEROVINGIAN TREASURE

THE Merovingians took much treasure from the Visigoths when they drove them into Spain, or acquired it from Visigothic brides like Galswinth and Brunhild, when those fairy-tale princesses arrived in silver carriages, bringing immense wealth with them as dowries to their husbands. This treasure is very relevant to the present day for a strange reason.

The story begins a few years before 1900 when a handsome French priest, Béranger Saunière, was given a small parish among the hills in the far south of France, Rennes-le-Château, a village situated where a powerful Visigothic city, Aereda, had once stood. It is about twenty miles from Carcassonne. The church was falling

to pieces, the few villagers and peasants were desperately poor. Among the tombstones and flat slabs in the churchyard was a carved slab bearing the effigy of a Merovingian king, Dagobert II, holding his infant son Sigibert, on horseback. This king was the grandson of Dagobert I who was considered the last strong Merovingian ruler. Dagobert II, who had been canonized, and his little son were assassinated in 679 A.D., which may account for the effigy having been lovingly carved in commemoration.

Soon Father Saunière began to repair his crumbling church. He discovered that one of the four pillars supporting the collapsing altar was hollow and contained four ancient parchments. These were written in strange codes so he took them to his nephew, director of the Seminary of St. Sulpice in Paris and a specialist in old documents. After a week's work the nephew returned Saunière's parchments with his findings. Back at Rennes-le-Château the priest began behaving like a man who had come into a fortune. He was generous to his poor parishioners, giving them piped water to their cottages and constructing a modern road through the village out of an old rough track. He built a handsome house with a fine garden for himself, which he called the Villa Bethany; he restored and redecorated his church on a lavish scale. He also erected a tower, La Tour Magdala, from which he could watch the whole countryside whenever he wished. To one fellow priest he gave a beautiful ancient chalice and to another some coins dating back to Merovingian times, so he was certainly open-handed with his new-found wealth.

In spite of all this Father Saunière took great pains to conceal the source of his riches. He would disappear for hours among the local hills, saying that he was just collecting rocks. He removed the markings on a tomb slab

of the Countess of Blanchfort, the ruins of whose castle
are still a local landmark. The noble Blanchfort family
and their castle go back to ancient times. However someone collecting tomb inscriptions fortunately copied the
lettering. Two of the precious parchments have vanished, but two still remain.

If the priest removed some evidence he left a whole
new set of clues when he rebuilt his little church. The
Christ in Glory over the altar he painted himself and it
contains many local pointers, including the tomb and
ruins of the Blanchfort castle. He invited an artist to
paint the fourteen Stations of the Cross to his design and
these are full of baffling clues. On a pillar he carved the
year of his discovery, 1891, but the pillar itself dates
from Visigothic times, when these tribes swept across
Europe and eventually sacked Rome in 410 A.D. It was
here that they captured the Treasure of the Temple of
Solomon, a treasure 'adorned for the most part with
emeralds', according to Procopius the historian. The
Treasure of Jerusalem had been brought to Rome in 70
A.D. by the Emperor Titus and this event is recorded on
Titus' Arch in Rome.

After that the Visigoths carried the booty into southern France as far as Toulouse, which was conquered in
507 by Clovis, the Merovingian king, who pursued the
fleeing enemy down into Spain. The Visigoths managed
to save some of the treasure and bring it to Toledo, but
some was captured by Clovis. We know that when the
Visigothic princesses, Brunhild and Galswinth left
Toledo to marry their royal Merovingian husbands they
brought dowries with them of immense value.

Father Saunière disappeared from the story. He made
a confession to another priest who was said to be white
and shaken, and unable to smile again for some months.
In 1917 Saunière himself died of a stroke without speak-

ing. All his possessions were found to be in the name of Marie his housekeeper, who lived in comfort until her own death in 1953. Presumably she knew his secrets but he had become paralysed and could reveal nothing.

Now there are scholars hard at work on all these silent clues. The French government is cautious and has forbidden excavations at Rennes-le-Château. Recently someone secretly smashed the defaced tomb slab of the Countess of Blanchfort. Did he hope to find untold wealth within this grave?

So we see in this strange jig-saw puzzle of history how these ancient Frankish kings are brought into elusive contact with us today. Their conquests, their marches, their expeditions, their marriages to lovely princesses, are all relevant to this treasure-hunt, which continues in a forgotten corner of southern France in our own time. Let us hope that the mystery can be solved before too many years go by.

INDEX

HOW YOU BEGAN
AMABEL WILLIAMS-ELLIS 30p

552 54064 1   Carousel Non Fiction

You began from a tiny blob of jelly, smaller than the full stop on this page. This book provides a simple but comprehensive account of the beginnings of human beings and other creatures which have developed over the centuries.

HOKE'S JOKES, CARTOONS AND FUNNY THINGS
by HELEN HOKE   20p

552 54063 3   Carousel Non Fiction

Every page of this book is packed with colourful cartoons, jokes and riddles.

TALES TOLD BY THE FOSSILS   CAROLL LANE FENTON

Vol. 1: UNEARTHING LIFE'S PAST   552 54046 3

30p each

Carousel Non Fiction

This volume explains what fossils are, how they are found and how they divide the earth's history into an orderly series of ages.

Vol 2: FROM DINOSAURS TO MAN   552 54047 1

Traces the history of life from the late Triassic period, 230 million years ago when lizard-hipped dinosaurs lived, up until 100,000 years ago, when mankind had developed from ape-man to Neanderthal man.

HOW & WHY WONDER BOOK OF FOSSILS 30p

552 86564 8

This is a comprehensive study of fossils, expertly illustrated and easy to follow. The author is an ardent naturalist and conservationist.

PINOCCHIO Carlo Collodi 35p

552 52053 5 Carousel Fiction

This is a lovely edition of this famous story of Geppetto's piece of wood that comes alive. It contains many marvellous photographs from the A.T.V. television series.